VIRGO
WITCH
♍

©JAMES C. WELCH

Ivo Dominguez, Jr. (Georgetown, DE) has been active in the magickal community since 1978. He is one of the founders of Keepers of the Holly Chalice, the first Assembly of the Sacred Wheel coven. He currently serves as one of the Elders in the Assembly. Ivo is the author of several books, including *The Four Elements of the Wise* and *Practical Astrology for Witches and Pagans*. In his mundane life, he has been a computer programmer, the executive director of an AIDS/HIV service organization, a bookstore owner, and many other things. Visit him at www.ivodominguezjr.com.

About the Authors

© BRIAN WYCOFF

Thumper (Horkos) Marjorie Splitfoot Forge is a Gardnerian High Priest, an initiate of the Minoan Brotherhood, an Episkopos of the Dorothy Clutterbuck Memorial Cabal of Laverna Discordia, a recovering alcoholic, and a notary public from Houston, Texas. By day, he manages a leather and fetishwear shop, and by night, he dabbles in Chaos Magic, offers geomantic and lithomantic readings, and blogs irreverently. His essays have previously appeared in *The Gorgon's Guide to Magical Resistance* (Revelore Press, 2022) and *Modern Witchcraft with the Greek Gods: History, Insights & Magickal Practice* (Llewellyn Publications, 2022). You can visit him online at https://ThumperForge.com and www.patheos.com /blogs/FivefoldLaw.

VIRGO
WITCH

♍

IVO DOMINGUEZ, JR.
THUMPER FORGE

Llewellyn Publications
Woodbury, Minnesota

FIRST EDITION
First Printing, 2023

Art direction and cover design by Shira Atakpu
Book design by Christine Ha
Interior art by the Llewellyn Art Department
Tarot Original 1909 Deck © 2021 with art created by Pamela Colman Smith and Arthur Edward Waite. Used with permission of LoScarabeo.
The Virgo Correspondences appendix is excerpted with permission from *Llewellyn's Complete Book of Correspondences: A Comprehensive & Cross-Referenced Resource for Pagans & Wiccans* © 2013 by Sandra Kynes.

Llewellyn Publications is a registered trademark of Llewellyn Worldwide Ltd.

Library of Congress Cataloging-in-Publication Data (Pending)
ISBN: 978-0-7387-7285-1

Llewellyn Worldwide Ltd. does not participate in, endorse, or have any authority or responsibility concerning private business transactions between our authors and the public.
    All mail addressed to the author is forwarded but the publisher cannot, unless specifically instructed by the author, give out an address or phone number.
    Any internet references contained in this work are current at publication time, but the publisher cannot guarantee that a specific location will continue to be maintained. Please refer to the publisher's website for links to authors' websites and other sources.

Llewellyn Publications
A Division of Llewellyn Worldwide Ltd.
2143 Wooddale Drive
Woodbury, MN 55125-2989
www.llewellyn.com

Printed in the United States of America

Other Books by Ivo Dominguez, Jr.

The Four Elements of the Wise
Keys to Perception: A Practical Guide to Psychic Development
Practical Astrology for Witches and Pagans
Casting Sacred Space
Spirit Speak

Other Books in The Witch's Sun Sign Series

Aries Witch
Taurus Witch
Gemini Witch
Cancer Witch
Leo Witch
Libra Witch
Scorpio Witch
Sagittarius Witch
Capricorn Witch
Aquarius Witch
Pisces Witch

CONTENTS

SPELLS, RECIPES, AND PRACTICES

Ivo Dominguez, Jr.

This is the sixth book in the Witch's Sun Sign series. There are twelve volumes in this series with a book for every Sun sign, but with a special focus on witchcraft. This series explores and honors the gifts, perspectives, and joys of being a witch through the perspective of their Sun sign. Each book has information on how your sign affects your magick and life experiences with insights provided by witches of your Sun sign, as well as spells, rituals, and practices to enrich your witchcraft. This series is geared toward helping witches grow, develop, and integrate the power of their Sun sign into all their practices. Each book in the series has ten writers, so there are many takes on the meaning of being a witch of a particular sign. All the books in the Witch's Sun Sign series are a sampler of possibilities, with pieces that are deep, fun, practical, healing, instructive, revealing, and authentic.

Welcome to the Virgo Witch

I'm Ivo Dominguez, Jr., and I've been a witch and an astrologer for over forty years. In this book, and in the whole series, I've written the chapters focused on astrological information and collaborated with the other writers. For the sake of transparency, I am a Sagittarius, and most of the nine other writers for this book are Virgos.[1] The chapters focused on the lived experience of being a Virgo witch were written by my coauthor, Thumper Forge, who is a Gardnerian High Priest, an initiate of the Minoan Brotherhood, a Discordian, and a recovering alcoholic. The spells and shorter pieces written for this book come from a diverse group of strong Virgo witches. Their practices will give you a deeper understanding of yourself as a Virgo and as a witch. With the information, insights, and methods offered here, your Virgo nature and your witchcraft will be better united. The work of becoming fully yourself entails finding, refining, and merging all the parts that make your life and identity. This all sounds very serious, but the content of this book will run from lighthearted to profound to do justice to the topic. Moreover, this book has practical suggestions on using the power of your Sun sign to improve your craft as a witch. There are many

---

1. The exceptions are Dawn Aurora Hunt, who contributes a recipe for each sign in the series, and Sandra Kynes, whose correspondences are listed in the appendix.

books on Virgo or astrology or witchcraft; this book is about wholeheartedly being a Virgo witch.

There is a vast amount of material available in books, blogs, memes, and videos targeted at Virgo. The content presented in these ranges from serious to snarky, and a fair amount of it is less than accurate or useful. After reading this book, you will be better equipped to tell which of these you can take to heart and use, and which are fine for a laugh but not much more. There is a good chance that you will be flipping back to reread some chapters to get a better understanding of some of the points being made. This book is meant to be read more than once, and some parts of it may become reference material that you will use for years. Consider keeping a folder, digital or paper, for your notes and ideas on being a Virgo witch.

What You Will Need

Knowing your Sun sign is enough to get quite a bit out of this book. However, to use all the material in this book, you will need your birth chart to verify your Moon sign and rising sign. In addition to your birth date, you will need the location and the time of your birth as exactly as possible. If you don't know your birthtime, try to get a copy of your birth certificate, though not all birth certificates list times. If it is reasonable and you feel comfortable, you can ask family members for information. They may remember an exact time, but even narrowing it down to a range of hours will be useful.

There is a solution to not having your exact birth time. Since it takes moments to create birth charts using software, you can run birth charts that are thirty minutes apart over the span of hours that contain your possible birth times. By reading the chapters that describe the characteristics of Moon signs and rising signs, you can reduce the pile of possible charts to a few contenders. Read the descriptions and find the chart whose combination of Moon sign and rising sign rings true to you.

There are more refined techniques that a professional astrologer can use to get closer to a chart that is more accurate. However, knowing your Sun sign, Moon sign, and rising sign is all you need for this book. There are numerous websites that offer free basic birth charts that you can view online. For a fee, more detailed charts are available on these sites.

You may want to have an astrological wall calendar or an astrological day planner to keep track of the sign and phase of the Moon. You will want to keep track of what your ruling planet, Mercury, is doing. Over time as your knowledge grows, you'll probably start looking at where all the planets are, what aspects they are making, and when they are retrograde or direct. You could do this all on an app or at a website, but it is often easier to flip through a calendar or planner to see what is going on than entering and selecting a date at a time. Flipping forward and back through the weeks and months ahead can give you a better sense of how to prepare for upcoming celestial influences. Moreover, the calendars and planner contain basic background information about astrology and are a great start for studying astrology.

You're a Virgo and So Much More

Every person is unique, complex, and a mixture of traits that can clash, complement, compete, or collaborate with each other. This book focuses on your Virgo Sun sign and provides starting points for understanding your Moon sign and rising sign. It cannot answer all your questions or be a perfect fit because of all the other parts that make you an individual. However, you will find more than enough to enrich and deepen your witchcraft as a Virgo. There will also be descriptions that you won't agree with or that you think do not portray you. In some instances, you will be correct, and in other cases, you may come around to acknowledging that the information does apply to you. Astrology can be used for magick, divination, personal development, and more. No matter what the purpose, your understanding of astrology will change over time as your life unfolds and your experience and self-knowledge broaden. You will probably return to this book several times as you find opportunities to use more of the insights and methods.

This may seem like strange advice to find in a book for the Virgo witch, but remember that you are more than a Virgo witch. In the process of claiming the identity of being a witch, it is common to want to have a clear and firm definition of who you are. Sometimes this means overidentifying with a category, such as water witch, herb witch, crystal witch, kitchen witch, and so on. It is useful to become aware of the affinities that you have so long as you do not limit and bind yourself to being less than you are. The best use for this book is to uncover all the parts of you that are Virgo so you can integrate them well. The finest witches I know have well-developed specialties but also are well rounded in their knowledge and practices.

Onward!

With all that said, the Sun is the starting point for your power and your journey as a witch. The first chapter is about the profound influence your Sun sign has, so don't skip through the table of contents; please start at the beginning.

After that, Thumper will dive into magick and practices that come naturally to Virgo witches. I'll be walking you through the benefits of picking the right times, places, and things to energize your Virgo magick. Thumper will also share a couple of real-life personal stories on his ups and downs, as well as advice on the best ways to protect yourself spiritually and set good boundaries when you really need to. I'll introduce you to how your Moon sign and your rising sign shape your witchcraft. Thumper offers great stories about how his Virgo nature comes forward in his life as a witch, and then gives suggestions on self-care and self-awareness. I'll share a full ritual with you to call on the spirit of your sign. Lastly, Thumper offers his wisdom on how to become a better Virgo witch. Throughout the whole book, you'll find tables of correspondences, spells, recipes, techniques, and other treasures to add to your practices.

HOW YOUR SUN
POWERS YOUR MAGICK

Ivo Dominguez, Jr.

The first bit of astrology people generally learn is their Sun sign. Some enthusiastically embrace the meaning of their Sun sign and apply it to everything in their life. They feel their Sun is shining and all is well in the world. Then at some point they'll encounter someone who will, with a bit of disdain, enlighten them on the limits of Sun sign astrology. They feel their Sun isn't enough, and they scramble to catch up. What comes next is usually the discovery that they have a Moon sign, a rising sign, and all the rest of the planets in an assortment of signs. Making sense of all this additional information is daunting as it requires quite a bit of learning and/or an astrologer to guide you through the process. Wherever you are on this journey into the world of astrology, at some point you will circle back around and rediscover that the Sun is still in the center.

The Sun in your birth chart shows where life and spirit came into the world to form you. It is the keeper of your spark of spirit and the wellspring of your power. Your Sun is in Virgo, so that is the flavor, the color, the type of energy that is at your core. You are your whole birth chart, but it is your Virgo Sun that provides the vital force that moves throughout all parts of your life. When you work in harmony and alignment with your Sun, you have access to more life and the capacity to live it better. This is true for all people, but this advice takes on a special meaning for those who are witches. The root of a witch's magick power is revealed by their Sun sign. You can draw on many kinds of energy, but the type of energy you attract with greatest ease is Virgo. The more awareness and intention you apply to connecting with and acting as a conduit for that Virgo Sun, the more effective you will be as a witch.

The more you learn about the meaning of a Virgo Sun, the easier it will be to find ways to make that connection. To be effective in magick, divination, and other categories of workings, it is vital that you understand yourself—your motivations, drives, attractions—so you can refine your intentions, questions, and desired outcomes. Understanding your Sun sign is an important step in that process. One of the goals shared by both witchcraft and astrology is to affirm and to integrate the totality of your nature to live your best life. The glyph for the Sun in astrology is a dot with a circle around it. Your Virgo Sun is the dot and the circle, your center, and your circumference. It is your beginning and your journey. It is also the core of your personal Wheel of the Year, the seasons of your life that repeat, have resonances, but are never the same.

How Virgo Are You?

The Sun is the hub around which the planets circle. Its gravity pulls the planets to keep them in their courses and bends space-time to create the place we call our solar system. The Sun in your birth chart tugs on every other part of your chart in a similar way. Everything is both bound and free, affected but seeking its own direction. When people encounter descriptions of Virgo traits, they will often begin to make a list of which things apply to them and which don't. Some will say that they are the epitome of Virgo traits, others will claim that they are barely Virgo, and many will be somewhere in between. Evaluating how closely or not you align with the traditional characteristics of a Virgo is not a particularly useful approach to understanding your sign. If you are a Virgo, you have all the Virgo traits somewhere within you. What varies from person to person is the expression of those traits. Some traits express fully in a classic form, others are blocked from expressing or are modified, and sometimes there is a reaction to behave as the opposite of what is expected. As a Virgo, and especially as a witch, you have the capacity to activate dormant traits, to shape functioning traits, and to tone down overactive traits.

The characteristics and traits of signs are tendencies, drives, and affinities. Gravity encourages a ball to roll down a hill. A plant's leaves will grow in the direction of sunlight. The warmth of a fire will draw people together on a cold night. A flavor you enjoy will entice you to take another bite of your food. Your Virgo Sun urges you to be and to act like a Virgo. That said, you also have free will and volition to make other choices. Moreover, the rest of your birth chart and the ever-changing celestial influences are also shaping your options, moods, and drives. The more you become aware of the traits and behaviors that come with being a Virgo, the easier it will be to choose how you express them. Most people want to have the freedom to express to make a difference in the world, but for a Virgo, this is essential for their well-being.

As a witch, you have additional tools to work with the Virgo energy. You can choose when to access and how you shape the qualities of Virgo as they come forth in your life. You can summon the energy of Virgo, name the traits you desire, and manifest them. You can also banish or neutralize or ground what you don't need. You can find where your Virgo energy short-circuits, where it glitches, and unblock it. You can examine your uncomfortable feelings and your less-than-perfect behaviors to seek the shadowed places within so you can heal or integrate them. Virgo is a spirit and a current of collective consciousness that is vast in size. Virgo is also a group mind and archetype. Virgo is not limited to humanity; it engages with plants, animals, minerals, and all the physical and nonphysical beings of the Earth and all its associated realms. As a witch, you can call upon and work with the spiritual entity that is Virgo. You can live your life as a ritual. The motion of your life can be a dance to the tune and rhythm of the heavens.

The Virgo Glyph

The glyph for Virgo has a few variants but they all contain a shape that resembles the letter *M* and an additional curve or loop that crosses over the third stem of the letter. The Virgo glyph can be seen

as spiritual force descending into manifestation then rising and repeating the process until it comes to the crossroads of choice. It also resembles the intestines, the absorption of nutrients that is ruled by Virgo. In the pictographic code of the astrological glyphs, vertical lines connect the above and the below, circles and loops represent spirit, and semicircles represent soul. Spirit is the part of you that is eternal, and soul is the part that is shaped and changed by the experiences of incarnation. The glyph for Virgo tells a story of the complicated journey and relationship between spirit and matter, heaven and earth. The glyph speaks of the care needed to navigate when they fall out of sync and become a tangle or become a crossroads that begs the question of a direction. Your life is about mapping the best course and picking the best available outcomes.

With the use of your imagination, you can see this glyph as hair ready to be brushed and unknotted. The shape of the glyph can also remind you of waves of power spreading outward, hitting a barrier, and rebounding upon themselves. This glyph is the chart or graph that shows how the ideal interacts with the real. It is Virgo's job to be the oracle of the graph that reads the signs, collects the data, and produces a pragmatic reading. The closer you look at the glyph and contemplate it, the more you see. Virgo's gift is to see with both microscopic and telescopic vision.

By meditating on the glyph, you will develop a deeper understanding of what it is to be a Virgo. You may also come up with your own personal gnosis or story about the glyph that can be a key that is uniquely yours. The glyph for Virgo can be used as a sigil to call or concentrate its power. The glyph for Virgo can be used in a similar fashion to the scribing of an invoking pentacle that is used to open the gates to the elemental realms. However, instead of the elemental realms, this glyph opens the way to the realm of heart and spirit that is the source of Virgo. To make this glyph work, you need to deeply ingrain the feeling of scribing this glyph. Visually it is a simple glyph, so memorizing it is easy, but having a kinesthetic feel for it turns it into magick. Spend some time doodling the glyph on paper. Try drawing the glyph on your palm with a finger for several repetitions as that adds several layers of sensation and memory patterns.

Whenever you need access to more of your magickal energy, scribe the Virgo glyph in your mind, on your hand, in the air, however you can. Then pull, channel, and feel your center fill with whatever you need. It takes very little time to open this connection using the glyph. Consider making this one of the practices you use to get ready to do divination, spell work, ritual, or just to start your day.

Virgo Patterns

This is a short list of patterns, guidelines, and predilections for Virgo Sun people to get you started. If you keep a book of shadows, or a journal, or files on a digital device to record your thoughts and insights on magickal work, you may wish to create your own list to expand upon these. The process of observing, summarizing, and writing down your own ideas in a list is a great way to learn about your sign.

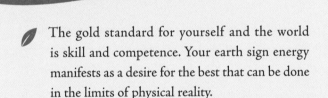

- The gold standard for yourself and the world is skill and competence. Your earth sign energy manifests as a desire for the best that can be done in the limits of physical reality.

- For Virgo, the devil is in the details, but so is the divine. You are sure that if you fix the right details, the ideal will become manifest as the real.

- *Virgo* means "virgin" in the old sense of having personal autonomy and being in charge of your own life rather than being chaste.

Virgo means "virgin" in the sense of being pure, entirely and truly yourself, and sexuality isn't impure unless you make it so.

Virgo is often represented as a goddess bearing a sheaf of grain. This is a summary of the Virgoan drive to create civilization and preserve the best parts of tradition. Think of a blend between Athena, Demeter, and Hestia, and that approximates the pattern of Virgo.

You tend to become fully immersed and engaged in your tasks, but if there is not enough progress toward perfection, you may abandon them and walk away. Make it a goal to manage frustration by finding a balance so that it is not all or nothing.

Sometimes Virgos are characterized as being aloof, fussy, or prudish. Although that may be true for some, it is generally not an accurate depiction. You analyze and evaluate things so that you can make informed choices. You keep your distance until you understand what is going on and whether you wish to take part.

Most Virgos do tend to judge themselves and their actions too strictly. Being conscientious and striving for improvement is not achieved through an abundance of self-blame. Offer yourself some space and grace.

You are mutable earth, so you can change and adapt. There are things you can change and things that you cannot change in yourself or the world. You have the power to adapt, but you must choose to do so because adaptation is not automatic and must be accepted.

You may have read lists of Virgo traits that emphasize service, work, and duty, and feel slightly stereotyped. Here's a richer and I believe truer depiction: Virgo wants to do work that matters, betters the world, and shows their strength and capacities.

What is your relationship with your physical health? Although this is a valuable question for everyone, it is particularly important for a Virgo. Your body is very selective when it comes to food, rest, and exercise. Your mind is always fretting about something, and your body is always listening to those thoughts and feelings. Virgos can be paragons of health or quite frail and you have a great deal of capacity to better your health.

Managing your body image is essential as well. All earth signs, and especially Virgos, are trying to bring the spiritual into the physical. You are a divine being, and don't doubt that for a second.

Your careful observation of the world started when you were a child. It is probable that you observed and became aware of some unpleasant things about the world long before you were able to understand and process them. Tending to your inner child, self-care, and reframing your past will make you happier and healthier.

You are not happy with wasted time in general, but when it is a result of other people's drama, you have little tolerance. Take it as an opportunity to gather data so you can prevent or plan around the next outbreak of common human frailties.

The amount varies from Virgo to Virgo, but alone time is as important to you as breathing.

Honesty is the best foundation for all that you build for yourself and others. You have a natural drive toward honesty, but what you need to develop is vocabulary and eloquence to clearly communicate your truths and listen to other people's truths.

The more you learn to appreciate and love yourself, the more energy you'll have to get the world in order. You'll also be seen as kinder and wiser instead of just disciplined and meticulous.

You understand the value of history, traditions, and that you stand on the shoulders of those who came before you. There is a tension between sticking to what has been proven to work and your desire to refine and improve all that you touch. Find ways to offer respect to the past while you craft a better way for the future.

Mutable Earth

The four elements come in sets of three. The modalities known as cardinal, fixed, and mutable are three different flavors or styles of manifestation for the elements. The twelvefold pattern that is the backbone of astrology comes from the twelve combinations produced from four elements times  three modalities. As you go around the wheel of the zodiac, the order of the elements is always fire, earth, air, then water, while the modalities are always in the order of cardinal, fixed, then mutable. Each season begins in the cardinal modality, reaches its peak in the fixed modality, and transforms to the next season in the mutable modality. The cardinal modality is the energy of creation bursting forth, coming into being, and spreading throughout the world. The fixed modality is the harmonization of energy so that it becomes and remains fully itself and is preserved. The mutable modality is the energy of flux that is flexibility, transformation, death, and rebirth.

Virgo is the sixth sign in the zodiac, so it is earth of the mutable modality. This is why a Virgo witch can call up power of inquiry and organization so quickly. As a Virgo witch, you can call upon earth in all its forms; it is easiest to draw upon mutable earth.

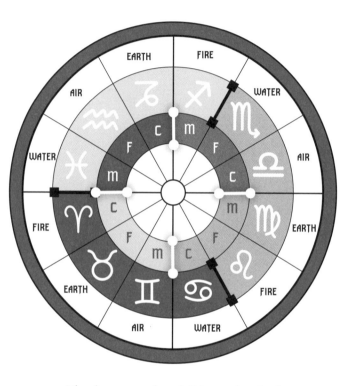

The elements and modalities on the wheel

Mercury, Your Ruling Planet

Your Sun sign determines the source and the type of energy that you have in your core. The ruling planet for a sign reveals your go-to moves and your intuitive or habitual responses for expressing that energy. Your ruling planet provides a curated set of prebuilt responses and custom-tailored stances for you to use in day-to-day life. The name of this planet may bring to mind the Greek Hermes or the Roman Mercury, the fleetfooted messengers of their pantheons. However, the planet Mercury and how it influences Virgo is about more than being a traveler, a herald, and a messenger. Since Virgo is an earth sign, this encourages the expression of Mercury to take a more physical and practical form. All deities related to crafts, record-keeping, and so on connect to Virgo through this earthy Mercury. The touch of Hephaestus, Brigid, and Thoth is here, as well as many others. Mercury's glyph suggests a scepter or a staff of office. Virgo likes to wield that scepter to bring order, pattern, and proper function to the material world.

Virgo witches are more strongly affected by whatever Mercury is doing in the heavens. It is useful to keep track of the aspects that Mercury is making with other planets. You can get basic information on what aspects mean and when they are happening in astrological calendars and online resources. You will feel Mercury retrogrades more strongly than most people, but you can find ways to make them useful periods to analyze what you've already done or to plan. Virgo witches will notice that the impact of the Mercury retrograde will start earlier and end a few days later than the listed duration. When Mercury in the heavens is in Virgo, you will feel an extra boost of energy. This first step to using the power of Mercury is to pay attention to what it is doing, how you feel, and what is happening in your life. Witches can shift their relationship with the powers that influence them. Your awareness of these powers makes it possible to harness those energies to purposes that you choose. Close your eyes, feel for that power, and channel it into your magick.

Mercury can be as great a source of energy for a Virgo witch as the element of earth. Although there is some overlap between the qualities and capacities assigned to Mercury and earth, the differences are greater. Mercury shapes how you form thoughts and words out of the stream of consciousness. Earth is the medium that forms the world that we perceive, think about, and shape. Mercury has the power to motivate or block your actions and to separate or join heart and mind. Earth is the ground of being that provides the experiences that are life. Mercury is all symbolic exchanges, not just communication. Mercury is commerce, sacred offerings, and the principle of reciprocity. Earth is the principle of manifestation, order generated by attraction, contraction, and crystallization. Earth provides the limits that provoke wisdom. Over time, you can map out the overlapping regions and the differences between Mercury and earth. Using both planetary and elemental resources can give you a much broader range and more finesse.

Virgo and the Zodiacal Wheel

The order of the signs in the zodiac can also be seen as a creation story where the run of the elements repeats three times. Virgo is in the second third of the zodiac, the second run of the four elements in the story of the universe. Having come into existence, the goal of the elements at this point is to become fully themselves. Virgo remembers their purposes for coming into being. The earth of Virgo is changeable, rearrangeable, and transformative. It evaluates the possibilities of existence to find the optimal combinations. Although Virgo is sometimes stereotyped as being too reserved and standoffish, the deeper truth is that they truly understand what is at stake in the world and see the work that must be done. Although true for all witches, the Virgo witch needs to let go of self-doubt, choose to take risks, and draw from where their power dwells within them. When you can consistently connect with your Virgo nature that is your most authentic self, you become the power that can energize anything. You can make progress in this quest through meditation and inner journeys, but that alone will not do. The Virgo witch learns by doing, by practice, and by being productive in the world. When a Virgo witch connects to the spiritual qualities of earth, they become the sovereign that governs the constant state of change that is life and encourages evolution.

The sign and planet rulers on the zodiac wheel

VIRGO
CORRESPONDENCES

♍

Power: To Analyze

Keyword: Discernment

Roles: Planner, Healer, Judge

Ruling Planet: Mercury

Element: Mutable Earth

Colors: Green, Earth Tones, Neutrals

Shape: Octagon

Metals: Mercury, Aluminum, Platnium, Bronze

Body Part Ruled: Belly

Day of the Week: Wednesday

Affirmation:
*My goal is to be ever better,
but not to expect perfection.*

WITCHCRAFT THAT COMES NATURALLY TO A VIRGO

Thumper Forge

I *might* be a little biased here, but Virgos make the most awesome witches. We're analytical, focused, and goal-oriented, and while other signs tend to view us as control freaks, our desire to stay on top of everything can easily translate into magical prowess.

Following are some areas of occultism that fit snugly into the arsenal of the Virgo witch. I'm presenting them in alphabetical order, because to do otherwise would be the editorial equivalent of nails down a chalkboard. You are most welcome, fellow Virgos.

Binding

As Ivo once pointed out to me, the various plants associated with Virgo tend to sport vines and brambles, and as is often the case when it comes to magic, like does attract like. Ergo, Virgos bring a little something extra to the table when it comes to binding.

The scene in the 1996 movie *The Craft* in which protagonist Sarah casts a spell on antagonist Nancy nicely encapsulates the process of binding. While wrapping ribbon around a photo of Nancy, Sarah intones, "I bind you, Nancy, from doing harm; harm against other people, and harm against yourself."

Note that it wasn't "I curse you, Nancy"—Sarah didn't want to hurt her. But she also didn't want Nancy to hurt more people, and she didn't want Nancy doing further damage to her own psyche.

I've got nothing to prove it, but I firmly believe that Sarah was a Virgo, and I will die on this hill.

As we can see in the fictional rendering, bindings are protective as well as restrictive. And the mechanism is a little different than other types of coercive magic, in that in order to achieve results, the witch must also place the restrictions they're imposing on someone else upon themself.

Way back in the early 2000s, a series of sexual assaults occurred in the Bay Area of Northern California, and a group of witches decided to do something about it. Since all the attacks took place in the same location, the witches gathered there and performed a binding ritual against the unknown assailant, who was "coincidentally" identified and arrested the following afternoon.

And this is how I learned how binding really works. In order to power the spell, the witches who cast it renounced the ability to cause harm with their genitals, thus binding the rapist from causing any further harm with his.

That right there is the key to effective binding. We're not just tying a person up with metaphorical string—we're preventing them from taking a certain course of action by relinquishing the ability to pursue that course of action ourselves. For instance, if I'm going to bind someone from spreading rumors about me, I'm also binding myself from spreading rumors about them. It's basically a spiritual quid pro quo.

And even though the practice does kind of toe the line of what some would call "baneful" magic, there are a number of benevolent ways to use binding. If you've got a pet with a penchant for wandering off, bind their collar with a bow of brown string to keep them close to home. If you've got a schedule that you've absolutely got to keep, try binding it to lock it into place. If a friend is suffering from a broken bone, get a poppet (or doll, or action figure) that resembles them and bind the affected body part with white gauze to promote healing.

One last word on the subject: Regardless of my own background with this kind of work, and the obvious potential for both good and mischief, I am not here to dictate ethical principles to you. If your personal moral code prohibits you from casting binding spells, for whatever reason, that is totally okay; and if your personal moral code allows for the use of binding magic, that is also totally okay.

Follow your Virgo heart, and you will successfully put a bow on it.

Herbalism

As earth signs, Virgo witches are naturally drawn to the magic of herbs and plants. However, we're often stymied by the Virgo impulse to try to learn everything all at once, which leads to gnashing of teeth and throwing in towels when we don't become experts overnight.

Fortunately for us, the foundation of magical herbalism is simply quality over quantity. We absolutely do not need to worry about absorbing a vast database of herbal knowledge; instead, we can focus on a narrow selection of standard-issue herbs that will cover almost all our magical needs.

The rule of thumb when stocking up on herbs is akin to something the witch Athena tells Ted the Bellhop in the first scene of the movie *Four Rooms*: "Mostly what we need is from the kitchen." With that in mind, here are twelve herbs that every Virgo witch should have in their cupboard, all of which can be found reasonably priced at your friendly neighborhood Safeway:

- Allspice
- Basil
- Bay Leaf
- Chamomile
- Cinnamon
- Ginger

- Marjoram
- Mint
- Pepper
- Rosemary
- Thyme
- Vanilla

I don't want to get too heavily into specific attributes and correspondences, mainly because there are excellent resources out there that cover the topic much better than I ever could— my favorites being *Cunningham's Encyclopedia of Magical Herbs* by Scott Cunningham (Llewellyn Publications, 1985) and *The Treadwell's Book of Plant Magic* by Christina Oakley Harrington (Treadwell's, 2020). Suffice it to say, all these herbs have a variety of uses, and they can be mixed and matched in what I think of as "broad strokes" witchcraft:

- A sachet of basil, marjoram, and rosemary will make a home safe and peaceful.

- Allspice, cinnamon, and thyme will draw money.

- A bath with chamomile and mint will remove a hex.

- Add rose petals to ginger and vanilla to make a love charm.

- Throw black and red pepper in with some salt to banish the crap out of ne'er-do-wells.

There are other common herbs that come in handy for more tailored work, but if you need to cast a spell *right this very second*, at least one of the above will get the job done.

Most of these herbs can be found in the Spices and Seasonings aisle, except for chamomile and mint—for those, you can bop over to Coffee and Tea. (Just make sure you're getting a tisane that's nothing but chamomile or mint, versus a blend with multiple ingredients. Fun fact: valerian, which is often included with chamomile for nighttime teas, is historically used to make pacts with demons. You can totally still drink it to treat insomnia, but maybe don't chant any Latin while it's brewing.)

The only must-have herb not on this list is lavender. It's not normally available at the grocer's, but it's still easy to find and multipurpose as all get-out, plus it can take the place of pretty much anything you don't have on hand. Casting a love spell? Lavender. Warding against the evil eye? Lavender. It's basically the Swiss Army knife of the herbal world and always worth having around.

Lithomancy

With Mercury as our ruling planet, Virgos are absolute aces at divination. Although the major challenge we face with that is determining which system of divination will click for us.

Personally, I love tarot, and … okay, wait, let me rephrase that. I love the idea of tarot. But I can't read tarot to save my damn life. I have tried to learn, and I've spent far too much money over the years searching for cards I could interpret without anguish, but I finally had to give up and admit that tarot is not in my wheelhouse.

Part of the problem is what I want to get out of readings: I'm usually just looking for a succinct yes-no answer, or specific direction through a given quandary. The Virgo in me likes easily identifiable patterns, without a bunch of variables in the mix shifting meanings around—seriously, just tell me whether I should or should not do the thing, in unambiguous terms. I'm also way more likely to connect with something down-to-earth than anything abstract or ethereal.

For me, as a Virgo witch, this means lithomancy— divination with stones—which is just about as earthy as you can get.

Before we get too far into this, I want to point out that we're defining "stones" very loosely here. To begin practicing lithomancy, all we need is three small objects, fairly uniform in size and shape: one to represent yes, one to represent no, and one to act as our indicator. I started out with antique marbles, and eventually branched out into using gaming dice. You may want to go with actual stones that have specific astrological correspondences that appeal to you. Pebbles inscribed with symbols would totally work, too. Regardless, the only things that really matter when choosing your stones are that you can easily cup all three of them in your hands, and you can tell them apart without trouble.

The first step to lithomancy is creating a space in which to perform a reading: a consecrated cord formed into a small circle about a foot or so in diameter works well for this. It's also a good idea to have some padding under the cord if you've got it on a table, or some carpet or a rug underneath you if you're sitting on the floor, just to prevent your stones from chipping.

Think of a yes-no question, or a question phrased along the lines of "What will happen if ..." or "What will be the result of ..." then take up your stones, give them a shake, and cast them gently into the center of your circle. If your indicator lands closer to your yes stone, the answer is favorable; if it lands closer to your no stone, the answer is unfavorable. And if the indicator lands equidistant from the two other stones, your answer is maybe.

As simple a method as this might appear to be, a *lot* of information can be gleaned from the placements of the three stones. For instance, if the indicator lands smack next to yes, with no on the opposite side of your circle, then you've got an extremely strong yes as an answer. Or if no comes to rest directly between the indicator and yes, there are obstacles in the way of obtaining a favorable result.

Once you're getting consistently clear answers, you may want to incorporate other stones into your readings, to represent different areas of life, or even planetary and elemental influences. To further your studies, I highly recommend *Pagan Portals—The Art of Lithomancy: Divination with Stones, Crystals, and Charms* by Jessica Howard (Moon Books, 2022) and *Lithomancy: Divination and Spellcraft with Stones, Crystals, and Coins* by the Rev. Dr. Jon Saint Germain (Lucky Mojo Curio, 2018). Both books are brimming with cool info that I don't have the space to dive into here.

With some practice, and a growing sense of confidence in your intuition and abilities, you will be able to mine a surprising amount of insight out of a handful of nuggets scattered on your floor. And as a Virgo witch, you'll be divining the details in no time.

Oaths

One of the goddesses associated with Virgo is Dike, the Greek personification of human justice, order, and custom, and her influence has an undeniable impact on the collective virgin worldview. We have a strong sense of right and wrong, which spills into every area of our lives—there's the *correct* way of doing something, and there's how everyone *else* does it.

Were you a *Downton Abbey* fan? If so, you'll recall what Lady Mary said in the second episode of the first season, while watching Matthew struggle with dining and serving etiquette, "You'll get used to the way things are done here." You know how that line gave you a deep, satisfied thrill? That's because it was totally something Dike would say, and it resonated with Virgo witches.

This might seem like a liability at first glance, since witchcraft is far more gray than black or white, and what works for one practitioner may not be practical for another. But the upside is that when Virgo witches find the Craft that works for us, it *really* works—we take our magic seriously, and we commit to it.

This is also the reason why we thrive within initiatory traditions of witchcraft. Initiations usually come with oaths: things we swear to uphold when we become part of a tradition. Virgos don't give our word lightly, and we're known for our trustworthiness and reliability. So when we take an oath, we do everything in our power to keep it, which strengthens the tradition as a whole.

Initiatory traditions do tend to be coven-based, which, on the surface, may not look like a good fit for a Virgo. After all, how can we be expected to practice witchcraft with a group of people who may or may not know what they're doing … or, worse yet, may not know how *we* want things done? But any initiatory tradition is going to come with a ritual framework—guidelines, boundaries, and blueprints that delineate what is and is not part of the tradition. And Virgo witches freaking *flourish* inside frameworks: we're given clear indications of what is and is not expected of us; we know what our role and responsibilities are; and once we've earned the trust of our covenmates (and vice versa), we can relax our guard a little and work successfully with the witches around us.

Plus, our covenmates will have taken the same oaths that we have, which goes a long way toward easing our inherently high expectations of others.

Speaking of, those lofty standards of ours do come in handy in oathbound traditions, since Virgos tend to wind up in charge, whether we want to be or not. But in initiatory terms, this just means that we'll eventually be the ones administering the oaths, which is honestly second nature to us. In fact, if you *really* want to put your Virgo witchiness to good use, get commissioned as a notary public. (The procedure to obtain a notary commission varies from state to state, but it's usually not too onerous a process.) With stamp in hand, you'll get to spend your free time verifying identities, witnessing signatures, and administering oaths, which, from a mythological standpoint, will make you a representative of Dike on Earth. Even Lady Mary would be proud.

MAGICAL
CORRESPONDENCES
Thumper Forge

As we've discussed, Virgos are inherently adept at certain types of magic and witchcraft. Here are a few additional jumping-off points to inspire your own magical workings.

Some of these topics are covered earlier in this book, and some you may not be familiar with. (The hell is geomancy, anyway?) But all of them key into Virgo's natural talents and inclinations. Take a moment to review them and determine which ones might strike a chord with you. Then take some time to consider how you'd incorporate the ritual tools highlighted below into those particular workings and see what sort of Virgo witchcraft you can brew up.

Types of Spellcraft

+ Binding
+ Ceremonial magic
+ Chaos magic
+ Geomancy
+ Healing
+ Lithomancy

Magical Tools

- The wand (think of it as your personal caduceus)
- The pentacle
- Stones and crystals
- Salt
- Herbal and wood-based incenses
- Starlight

Magical Goals and Spell Ideas

- Eloquence
- Peaceful home
- Protection during travel
- Success in business
- Seeking clarity
- Uncovering secrets

Ivo Dominguez, Jr.

You've probably encountered plenty of charts and lists in books and online, cataloging which things relate to your Sun sign and ruling planet. There are many gorgeously curated assortments of herbs, crystals, music playlists, fashions, sports, fictional characters, tarot cards, and more that are assigned to your Sun sign. These compilations of associations are more than a curiosity or for entertainment. Correspondences are like treasure maps to show you where to find the type and flavor of power you are seeking. Correspondences are flowcharts and diagrams that show the inner occult relationships between subtle energies and the physical world. Although there are many purposes for lists of correspondences, there are two that are especially valuable to becoming a better Virgo witch. The first is to contemplate the meaning of the correspondences, the ways in which they reveal meaningful details about your Sun sign and ruling planet, and how they connect to you. This will deepen your understanding of what it is to be a Virgo witch. The second is to use these items as points of connection to access energies and essences that support your witchcraft. This will expand the number of tools and resources at your disposal for all your efforts.

Each of the sections in this chapter will introduce you to a type of correlation with suggestions on how to identify and use it. These are just starting points, and you will find many more as you explore and learn more. As you broaden your knowledge, you may find yourself a little bit confused as you find that sources disagree on the correlations. These contradictions are generally not a matter of who is in error but a matter of perspective, cultural differences, and the intended uses for the correlations. Anything that exists in the physical world can be described as a mixture of all the elements, planets, and signs. You may be a Virgo, but depending upon the rest of your chart, there may be strong concentrations of other signs and elements. For example, if you find that a particular herb is listed as associated with both Virgo and Gemini, it is because it contains both natures in abundance. In the cases of strong multiple correlations, it is important that you summon or tune in to the one that you need.

Times

You always have access to your power as a Virgo witch, but there are times when the flow is stronger, readily available, or more easily summoned. There are sophisticated astrological methods to select dates and times that are specific to your birth chart. Unless you want to learn quite a bit more astrology or hire someone to determine these for you, you can do quite well with simpler methods. Let's look at the cycles of the solar year, the lunar month, and the hours of day-night rotation. When the Sun is in Virgo, or the Moon is in Virgo, or it is late afternoon, you are in the sweet spot for tuning in to the core of your power.

Virgo season is roughly August 23 to September 22, but check your astrological calendar or ephemeris to determine when it is for a specific year in your time zone. The amount of energy that is accessible is highest when the Sun is at the same degree of Virgo as it is in your birth chart. This peak will not always be on your birth date but very close to it. Take advantage of Virgo season for working magick and for recharging and storing up energy for the whole year.

The Moon moves through the twelve signs every lunar cycle and spends around two and half days in each sign. When the Moon is in Virgo, you have access to more lunar power because the Moon in the heavens has a resonant link to the Sun in your birth chart. At some point during its time in Virgo, the Moon will be at the same degree as your Sun. For you, that will be the peak of the energy during the Moon's passage through Virgo that month. While the Moon is in Virgo, your psychism is stronger, as is your ability to manifest things. When the Moon is in its waning gibbous phase, in any sign, you can draw upon its power more readily because it is resonant to your sign.

None of the eight holidays in the Wheel of the Year are in Virgo season. None of the mutable signs anchors a holiday. The stations of the year, the holidays, are liminal times of transition. The mutable earth of Virgo is filled with change and transformation; it is liminal in a different way. Think about all the change that must happen in plants, animals, and the weather to set up the transition at the equinox. Virgo is the sixth sign of the zodiac, and the zodiac is like a clock. Late afternoon corresponds to the power of Virgo. If you are detail focused, you might be wondering when late afternoon is. This varies with the time of year and with your location, but if you must have a time, think of it as 4:00 p.m. to 6:00 p.m. Or you can use your intuition and feel your way to when afternoon is on any given day, when the slant of the Sun has become significant. The powers that flow during this time are rich, creative, and filled with possibilities for you to experience. Plan on using the Virgo energy of the late afternoon for inspiration and to feed spells for learning, divination, clarity, and change.

The effect of these special times can be joined in any combination. For example, you can choose to do work in the afternoon when the Moon is in Virgo, or the Sun is in Virgo in the late afternoon, or the Moon is in Virgo during Virgo season. You can combine all three as well. Each of these time period groupings will have a distinctive feeling. Experiment and use your instincts to discover how to use these in your work.

Places

There are activities, professions, phenomena, and behaviors that have an affinity, a resonant connection, to Virgo and its ruling planet, Mercury. These activities occur in the locations that suit or facilitate their expressions. There is magick to be claimed from those places that is earmarked for Virgo or your ruling planet, Mercury. Just like your birth chart, the world around you contains the influences of all the planets and signs, but in different proportions and arrangements. You can always draw upon Virgo or Mercury energy, though there are times when it is more abundant depending upon astrological considerations. Places and spaces have energies that accumulate and can be tapped like a battery. Places contain the physical, emotional, and spiritual environments that are created by the actions of the material objects, plants, animals, and people occupying those spaces. Some of the interactions between these things can generate or concentrate the energies and patterns that can be used by Virgo witches.

If you look at traditional astrology books, you'll find listings of places assigned to Virgo and Mercury that include locations such as these:

- Craft stores, woodshops, sewing rooms, where crafting happens
- Offices, IT departments, and mailrooms
- Health centers where bodywork, nutritional counseling, or yoga happens
- Farmers markets, plant nurseries, and garden centers
- Press pools, news centers, and editorial offices

These are very clearly linked to the themes associated with Virgo and Mercury. With a bit of brainstorming and free-associating, you'll find many other less obvious locations and situations where you can draw upon this power. For example, wherever chess or games of strategy (not chance) are being played, where weaving or fiber arts are being done, or where people are playing musical instruments can produce a current that you can plug into. Any situation where you use your intellect or dexterity to sort through or organize ideas, objects, or people, or engage in similar high-focus activities, can become a source of power for a Virgo witch. All implements or actions related to crafting, mending, writing, organizing, gardening, or specialty tools could also be sources for energy.

While you can certainly go to places that are identified as locations where Virgo and/or Mercury energy is plentiful to do workings, you can find those energies in many other circumstances. Don't be limited by the idea that the places must have a formalized link to Virgo. Be on the lookout for Virgo or Mercury themes and activities wherever you may be. Remember that people thinking, feeling, or participating in activities connected to your sign and its ruling planet are raising power. If you can identify with it as resonating with your Sun sign or ruling planet, then you can call the power and put it to use. You complete the circuit to engage the flow with your visualization, intentions, and actions.

Plants

Virgo is elegant, strives for health, loves peace, has integrity, and its colors are earthy greens, rich browns, and muted yellows and orange. Mercury augments a love of fine details, clarity of mind, management of emotions, and making connections between things. Herbs, resins, oils, fruits, vegetables, woods, and flowers that strongly exhibit one or more of these qualities can be called upon to support your magick. Here are a few examples:

- Holy basil (tulsi) because it relieves stress and nourishes the spirit.
- Lily of the valley for standing strong in your place in the world.
- Sweet pea for gratitude and steadfastness.
- Betony to dispel negativity and encourage grounded consciousness.
- Fennel for eloquence in speech and writing.

Once you understand the rationale for making these assignments, the lists of correspondences will make more sense. Another thing to consider is that each part of a plant may resonate more strongly with a different element, planet, and sign. Anise hyssop (*Agastache foeniculum*) shows its connection with Virgo and Mercury with its orderly leaves and because it is used to lift anxiety and promote honest communication. However, anise hyssop is also an herb of Venus used to draw people back together that have become estranged and reawaken your sense of beauty.

52

Which energy steps forward depends upon your call and invitation. "Like calls to like" is a truism in witchcraft. When you use your Virgo nature to make a call, you are answered by the Virgo part of the plant.

Plant materials can take the form of incense, anointing oils, altar pieces, potions, washes, magickal implements, foods, flower arrangements, and so on. The mere presence of plant material that is linked to Virgo or Mercury will be helpful to you. However, to gain the most benefit from plant energy, you need to actively engage with it. Push some of your energy into the plants and then pull on it to start the flow. Although much of the plant material you work with will be dried or preserved, it retains a connection to living members of their species. You may also want to reach out and try to commune with the spirit, the group soul, of the plants to request their assistance or guidance. This will awaken the power slumbering in the dried or preserved plant material. Spending time with living plants, whether they be houseplants, in your yard, or in a public garden, will strengthen your conversation with the green beings under Virgo's eye.

Crystals

Before digging into this topic, let's clear up some of the confusion around the birthstones for the signs of the zodiac. There are many varying lists for birthstones. Also be aware that some are related to the calendar month rather than the zodiacal signs. There are traditional lists, but the most commonly available lists for birthstones were created by jewelers to sell more jewelry. Also be cautious of the word *traditional* as some jewelers refer to the older lists compiled by jewelers as "traditional." The traditional lists created by magickal practitioners also diverge from each other because of cultural differences and the availability of different stones in the times and places the lists were created. If you have already formed a strong connection to a birthstone that you discover is not really connected to the energy of your sign, keep using it. Your connection is proof of its value to you in moving, holding, and shifting energy, whether or not it is specifically attuned to Virgo.

These are my preferred assignments of birthstones for the signs of the zodiac:

Aries	Bloodstone, Carnelian, Diamond
Taurus	Rose Quartz, Amber, Sapphire
Gemini	Agate, Tiger's Eyes, Citrine
Cancer	Moonstone, Pearl, Emerald

Leo	Heliodor, Peridot, Black Onyx
Virgo	Green Aventurine, Moss Agate, Zircon
Libra	Jade, Lapis Lazuli, Labradorite
Scorpio	Obsidian, Pale Beryl, Nuummite
Sagittarius	Turquoise, Blue Topaz, Iolite
Capricorn	Black Tourmaline, Howlite, Ruby
Aquarius	Amethyst, Sugalite, Garnet
Pisces	Ametrine, Smoky Quartz, Aquamarine

There are many other possibilities that work just as well, and I suggest you find what responds best for you as an individual. I've included all twelve signs in case you'd like to use the stones for your Moon sign or rising sign. Hands-on experimentation is the best approach, so I suggest visiting crystal or metaphysical shops and rock and mineral shows when possible. Here's some information on the three that I prefer for Virgo.

Green Aventurine
This stone offers gentle nudges to step out of your comfort zone and take your next step. It also soothes the nerves and

calms digestion. Green aventurine helps filter out and reduce that background noise of electromagnetic signals produced by the many electronic devices that fill modern life. This stone also helps increase mental focus when doing lengthy tasks. It has a long history of being a stone of luck, but what I think it really does is it helps you notice opportunities. Green aventurine's prodding for noticing things is also why it is known for showing people the beauty of the world. Aventurine comes in many colors, but the green version is best for Virgos.

Moss Agate

Moss agate is really a type of chalcedony that lets your overactive mind slow down and let go of tension. It is also known for bringing out your capacity for friendship and connecting with people. On the physical level, it helps reduce inflammation and remove toxins from the body. On the spiritual level, it helps you connect with your divine spark, your higher Self. Moss agate also helps moderate anger and frustration without dulling the drive to address the problem. This stone also promotes healthy gardens and fields and fosters fertility in the land. It can also help you communicate with nature spirits.

Zircon

It is one of the oldest crystals on the planet, with some dating back four billion years. It is a stone of eternity that can ground you deep into the power of the Earth. It can also connect you to higher planes because it remembers how it all started. Zircon is a crystal that helps remind us of our core values and authentic self. It is known as a stone that protects against the intrusion of negative spirits and magickal attacks. This crystal also helps you get the most out of rest and can help with sleep issues. Be aware that cubic zirconia is not zircon despite the similarity in the name.

Intuition and spiritual guidance play a part in the making of correlations, and in the case of traditional lore, the collective experience of many generations of practitioners. There is also reasoning behind how these assignments are made, and understanding the process will help you choose well. Here are some examples of this reasoning:

- Crystals assigned to Virgo are often earthy, understated, or elegant colors, and some have a subtle sparkle to them that is the Mercurial influence. Watermelon tourmaline and diopside are good examples for these assignments.

- Virgo's metal is mercury, a liquid metal that changes shape and conducts electricity. It is a highly toxic metal, so aluminum or platinum is its substitutes in most uses. Bronze, an alloy of copper, tin, and various other metals, is also associated with Virgo because it is a crafted metal of ancient lineage. Crystals such as jadeite and staurolite contain aluminum and are compatible with Virgo energy. Cinnabar is a stone that contains mercury and should be used with caution.

🍃 Crystals whose lore and uses are related to Virgo or Mercury actions or topics (clear communication, perseverance, strong focus, and healing) such as amazonite, rutilated smoky quartz, and unakite are recommended for Virgo.

🍃 Crystals that are the opposite of the themes for Virgo provide a counterbalance to an excessive manifestation of Virgo traits. For example, red jasper appears on lists of crystals for many other signs but is useful for Virgo as it brings fire and vitality to Virgo's cool nature.

🍃 Crystals suggested for Pisces, your opposite sign, are also useful to maintain your balance.

Working with Ritual Objects

A substantial number of traditions or schools of witch-craft use magickal tools that are consecrated to repre-sent and hold the power of the elements. Oftentimes in these systems, there is one primary tool for each of the elements and other tools that are alternatives to these or are mixtures of elements. There are many pos-sible combinations and reasons for why the elements are assigned to different tools in different traditions, and they all work within their own context. Find and follow what works best for you. Magickal tools and ritual objects are typically cleansed, consecrated, and charged to prepare them for use. In addition to follow-ing whatever procedure you may have for preparing your tools, add in a step to incorporate your energy and identity as a Virgo witch. This is especially productive for magickal tools and ritual objects that are connected to earth or are used to store, direct, or focus power. By adding Virgo energy and patterning into the prepara-tion of your tools, you will find it easier to raise, move, and shape energy with them in your workings.

There are many magickal tools and ritual objects that do not have any attachment to specific elements.

The core of your life force and magickal power springs from your Virgo Sun. So, when you consciously join your awareness of your Virgo core with the power flowing through the tools or objects, it increases their effectiveness. Adding your earthy energy does not make it an earth tool, it makes it a Virgo tool tuned to you. Use the name *Virgo*, its glyph, and its colors for imbuing objects with your power. Whether it be a pendulum, a wand, a crystal, or a chalice, your Virgo energy will be quick to rise and answer your call.

A Charging Practice

When you consciously use your Virgo witch energy to send power into tools, it tunes them more closely to your aura. Here's a quick method for imbuing any tool with your Virgo energy.

1. Place the tool in front of you on a table or altar.
2. Take a breath in, imagining that you are breathing in green energy, and then say "Virgo" as you exhale. Repeat this three times.
3. Place your hand on your lower belly with three fingers pointing down and spread.

Curl your pinky onto the nearest finger and tuck your thumb into your palm. You've just formed the glyph for Virgo over a part of the body it rules.

4. Now using a finger, trace the glyph of Virgo over or on the tool you are charging. Repeat this several times and imagine the glyph being absorbed by the tool.

5. Pick up the tool, take in a breath while imagining green energy, then blow that charged breath over the tool.

6. Say "Blessed be!" and proceed with using the tool or putting it away.

Hopefully this charging practice will inspire you and encourage you to experiment. Develop the habit of using the name *Virgo* as a word of power, the glyph for Virgo for summoning power, and the earthy colors of Virgo to visualize its flow. Feel free to use these spontaneously. Whether it be a pendulum, a wand, a crystal, a chalice, a ritual robe, or anything else that catches your imagination, these simple methods can have a large impact. The Virgo energy you imprint into objects will be quick to rise and answer your call.

HERBAL
CORRESPONDENCES

♍

These plant materials all have a special connection to your energy as a Virgo witch. There are many more, but these are a good starting point.

Herbs

Caraway	to banish negative beings and sharpen mental powers
Cypress	to make difficult changes
Dill	for legal victories and curse removal

Flowers

Jonquil	for new beginnings
Chrysanthemum	for resilience
Buttercups	to settle the emotions

Incense and Fragrances

Bayberry	to bring prosperity
Vertiver	for healing loss
Storax	for gaining hidden knowledge

CLEANSING AND SHIELDING

Thumper Forge

I feel like other Virgos are probably going to yell at me for saying this—if only because I'm exposing one of our secrets, and we *hate* that—but a lot of us are closeted slobs.

I know. We have this reputation as being neat and clean and persnickety about it, but behind the curtain, there are piles of dirty laundry and sinks full of dishes and *so much dust everywhere*. Like, if you snuck over to a Virgo's place right now and kicked open the door without warning, you'd find yourself facing an absolute crime scene of clutter and disarray, and the Virgo would be screaming, "I promise I was just about to take care of that!"

In fact, I spent a big chunk of my formative years steadfastly not believing in astrology, mainly because, in my mind, I didn't fit the Virgo stereotype. But then I started working at a music store, the manager of which being an occult enthusiast with way more knowledge of Things Astrological than I'd ever encountered.

(Note: For my Gen Z readers, a music store was where we used to go to buy compact discs, which contained music that we could listen to while hunting Wooly Mammoth and inventing the wheel.)

Once she learned of my budding interest in witchcraft, the manager took me under her wing and did her best to guide me along. We were chatting one day, and I mentioned that even though I did believe in magic and divination, I wasn't sold on astrology.

"Why is that?" she asked.

"Well, I'm a Virgo, and Virgos are supposed to be neat freaks. But I'm just kind of messy and disorganized."

She took a moment to think about that, then asked if I had a desk at home.

"I do," I said.

"What is it like? Does everything on your desk have its own place?"

"Everything does, actually," I said, surprised.

"And what happens if something gets out of place?"

"Well, then it's just *ruined*," I replied, a bit more forcefully than I'd intended.

She beamed in response. "Yeah. You're a Virgo."

And that's when I learned a key aspect of my Sun Sign. Yes, we Virgos are anal-retentive control freaks, but if anything goes askew in our carefully ordered little worlds, things can quickly go to pieces. And there can be some understandable shame around that.

We do, after all, hold ourselves to way higher standards than we'd hold anyone else to. So when things get out of order in our immediate environments, our natural inclination is to go, "Welp. It's no longer perfect. Clearly, I have failed at life." And then everything starts to feel overwhelming, and we look helplessly around our once pleasant homes while the narrator in our heads is like, "Tonight, on a very special episode of *Hoarders* …"

This is where cleansing comes in and why it's so important to Virgo witches. For us, physical cleansing and spiritual cleansing are pretty much the same thing; when we're physically clean, we feel spiritually clean.

The kicker is figuring out where to start, which, for me, can easily lead to an avalanche of despair. It's like, "I'm going to get this pile of books off the floor and back on the shelf where they belong. Except before I do that, I need to run a cloth over the bookshelf, which means I'll need to vacuum afterward, which means I need to move that hamper to get to the vacuum cleaner, although maybe I should do the laundry in the hamper first, except I'll need to pull stuff out of the dresser to have room for the clean clothes, so maybe I should make some space in the storage closet first, except I really don't want to see how packed it is in there, so you know what? I'm just going to watch B-rated horror movies for the next seven hours and pretend I live somewhere else."

Whenever I find myself sinking into this mindset, the first thing I do is go clean my altar. So let's start with yours as well.

I'm going to hazard a guess and say that your altar gets pretty dusty, because mine does—mainly because I get everything on it organized just so and am then reluctant to move any of it, for fear of not being able to get it back *exactly* in place. But it's also a small, manageable space that's easy to control.

First, let's take everything off of it. Wipe down the bare surface thoroughly—if you need to use a cleaning product, go with something citrus-based, since citrus fruits, especially lemon, break up stagnant conditions and remove negativity. Once the space is clean, turn to the objects you removed. Wipe each one down slowly and deliberately, meditating on where it came from, and why it's sacred to you. Once each object is dust-free, place it back on the altar, then repeat with the next object. Take all the time you need to do this—it's a space that's just for you, and it needs to feel correct.

When you have everything clean and where you want it, take a few moments to consider the final product. Does anything metal need to be polished, or anything old replaced? If so, get to work on that, and again, take all the time you need here, and get everything exactly the way you want it to be.

Once you're satisfied, kneel in front of your bright, fresh altar and light some incense—preferably a purifying wood, like cedar, juniper, or rowan, although sandalwood or frankincense would work just as well. Take one last moment to visualize the smoke as a manifestation of your cleaning efforts, and let it flow over and around you. Bask in the feeling of accomplishment. It feels pretty good, doesn't it?

As it turns out, we are nowhere near the failures we were starting to assume we are, and I am proud of us for accepting that. Now let's roll with the victory and go get those books off the floor.

Shielding

"What's this?" my partner at the time asked, pointing to a little red flannel bag hanging off the jamb of the front door.

"It's an herbal charm," I said. "From British folklore. It protects against thieves and lightning."

He responded with a long, blank stare.

"Have we been struck by lightning?" I asked.

Another pause. Then he begrudgingly admitted that we had not.

"Well, then," I said. "You're welcome."

Regardless of the state of the interior of my apartment, the place is warded to high heaven: there are witch bottles under the porch, and protective talismans in every window; a vintage goat ornament hangs by the back door, charged to mystically headbutt anyone who tries to enter without my permission; and a line of red brick dust lies in wait under the *nazar* welcome mat out front.

I mean, I *am* a Virgo witch, after all. I like to be prepared.

And it's funny, because as much effort as I put into magically protecting my home, you'd think I'd put the same amount of energy into shielding myself, but honestly, I don't. It's really an As Above, So Below situation—just as I'm far more likely to worry about other people's problems than my own, I'm much more inclined to shield my living space or my workplace than I am myself.

It's a pretty time-tested Virgo issue. We're coded to take care of other people, and it's easy for us to put precedence on others' well-being over our own. The upside to this is that we're loyal and helpful, and our friends can turn to us when they're in binds. But the downside is that we don't always have the reserves to take care of everyone else *and* ourselves, which means we can make unnecessary self-sacrifices without thinking about it.

The thing is, we have to be able to take care of ourselves if we're going to be of any use to the people around us—like how flight attendants tell you to put on your own oxygen mask before assisting anyone else with theirs. For Virgos, that means a very specific kind of shielding. Most people would call it setting healthy boundaries, but we're going to call it a filter.

When someone asks us for help, our natural inclination is to say yes, regardless of whether or not we're actually able to. Sometimes this looks like getting saddled with additional responsibilities at work that really shouldn't be ours, or agreeing to social commitments that we know we don't have the time or energy for. And we agree to these things, because we don't want to let anyone down. Or we worry that saying no will result in more problems for us to manage than if we just say yes and deal with it.

This is where our filter comes in. We need to be able to differentiate between reasonable and unreasonable requests, and we need our responses to be taken as kind but firm. And here's how we're going to get it up and running.

You will need two physical items to create your filter: a small piece of iron (a nail or screw would work well) and a piece of clear quartz. Iron is connected to the planet Saturn and represents restriction, whereas clear quartz is associated with active listening.

On a Saturday morning, right after you wake up, situate yourself in front of your altar or in a comfortable space in your home, and hold the piece of iron in your dominant hand and the piece of quartz in your receptive hand. Meditate on the metaphysical meanings of the items you're holding: restriction and listening. Picture those meanings as rings that slowly expand from your hands, eventually merging and continuing to grow, until there's one large ring around you, about two or three feet in diameter. Feel the ring spread out, over and under you, as if you're surrounded by a thin but sturdy egg-shaped screen.

The screen is going to refine what we hear, specifically when we're asked for assistance, so that we can differentiate between reasonable and unreasonable requests. For instance, let's say we're asked if we can come into work on our day off. Our gut instinct is going to be to say yes, regardless of whether we're actually able to. However, with our filter in place, we'll hear either, "This is a reasonable request," or, "This is not a reasonable request," and we can respond accordingly.

Our filter also acts as a binding in that it will prevent us from replying in such a way that we end up agreeing to things when we can't or don't want to do them. For instance, it may be instinctive for us to give reasons why we can't do the thing at the time it's being requested, which opens the door for negotiation: "Oh, you've got an obligation tomorrow morning? That's okay! You can just come in after that." Our filter binds against this, so regardless of what we automatically want to say, our response will be a solid "I'm afraid I'm not available, but thank you for thinking of me!"

And yes, I know this might seem more like spicy psychology than magic, but magic is all about changes in reality in accordance with will. The more we focus on our filter, the more change we enact in ourselves and the immediate world around us, until we're able to respond to requests succinctly and honestly, without stressing over how the requesters may perceive us or having to constantly maintain our newfound healthy boundaries.

And if you're like me and have possibly way too many wards around your home, you can use that to reinforce your filter. Imagine all those wards combining into a force field. As you walk out your door, feel a bit of that field bubble off and incorporate itself into your filter. It's a great way to add a little extra oomph to the work you've done to create your boundaries, and it'll turn the filter itself into a mini safe space to keep with you throughout the day.

It will also totally decrease the likelihood of you getting struck by lightning. Which may or may not have been an active fear in your head until I brought it up, but at least now you know you can take it off your plate.

Virgo New Moon Coffee Ritual

Mercedes NineMoons

Virgo, the Virgin Maiden, is a time to celebrate the wild freedom that is within all of us. I believe she is a Maiden with the wisdom of a Crone. I also believe Virgos carry a sense of strength like none other in the zodiac. The most important thing is *intention*, and Virgos have this in abundance. Virgo is all about renewal and work. This ritual uses that power to begin the new lunar phase with clarity and to set your intentions for the next cycle.

You will need:

+ A white or black candle
+ A tarot deck
+ Your preferred crystals
+ Sea salt and essential oils you like
+ Dark roast coffee, frankincense, mugwort, lavender, and charcoal for incense

Prepare a cleansing bath. Light a few candles (white) and add a few drops of oil (bergamot, lavender, jasmine make good choices) into the bathwater along with salt and dark roast coffee. Let the steam and heat release the fragrances and energy. Visualize the water and steam removing any negative energy and opening you to the energy of the new Moon. Then visualize green light entering through your feet from the Earth, going up to your head, and out into the universe.

At or around moonrise, pick a place to perform your ritual where you are comfortable, and if you can see the sky, all the better. Cleanse your space with incense made of ground coffee, frankincense, mugwort, and lavender on a charcoal.

Fill yourself with the Moon's energy. If you are working with spirits or deities, this would be a good time to cast a circle. I use the Cabot Traditional way to cast a circle; use whatever you know best.

Light your candle and set your crystals around it. You can chant or sing or recite an incantation that you find special. My personal incantation is this:

As the Moon changes, so shall I.
As the light becomes clear, so shall my path.
As the darkness fades, so shall the things that no longer
    serve me.
And so it is!

State your intentions for the upcoming lunar cycle. I believe in the power of intention and that All Is Mind, as said in *The Kybalion*. When we shape our thoughts, we shape our lives. New Moons are good for starting something new, to refocus your goals, or to reassess things that may or may not serve you.

Shuffle your tarot cards and lay out a three-card spread for past, present, and future.

+ *The Past:* What attitudes or feelings have shaped your intentions for this cycle? What habits do you need to break? What tools can you use going forward?

+ *The Present:* What forces are at work right now? Are there challenges that may hinder your progress? How far along your path are you?

+ *The Future:* What is your ideal outcome? What direction are you moving in? How can you manifest your intentions?

Take a few moments to reflect on the cards and how they correlate to your intentions, and what can you do to make sure your goals are met?

Close your ritual, snuff out your candle, and thank any deities or spirits you chose to work with.

WHAT SETS A VIRGO OFF, AND HOW TO RECOVER

Thumper Forge

So, what's the one simple thing that will cause a Virgo to devolve from a mild-mannered contributing member of society into a feral cat trapped in a dryer?

Trying to write a book during a Mercury retrograde. *Ask me how I know.*

Even though I don't really keep up with the myriad alignments of the planets and the stars—and honestly rarely know what day it actually is—I do make it a point to know when Mercury is going retrograde, since it signifies a period of unexpected delays, frustrations, and communication issues. Once Mercury goes retrograde, it is strongly recommended that one does not sign contracts, make important life decisions, plan trips, or tell arch, highbrow jokes that couldn't *possibly* offend anyone.

And don't even think about calling your mother. Just trust me on this one.

A planet is in retrograde when it appears to be moving backward through the zodiac. Planets don't actually move backward, of course. It just looks that way on account of a whole bunch of physics that I don't personally care to understand. Regardless, whenever a planet goes through a retrograde, the specific spheres of influence it governs go … well, splooey. As mutable earth signs ruled by Mercury, Virgos tend to go splooey along with them.

Virgo witches are nourished by consistency, but during a Mercury retrograde, our most treasured stabilities are in flux, and while we're normally very good at adapting, we end up adapting in the wrong directions. Like, if you've ever played volleyball, you've probably found yourself in a situation where the ball flies over the net, and three players yell, "Got it," and then they all think someone else is going to get it and step back, and the ball lands on the floor. If you can recall such an event, then you've got a good idea of what Virgos go through when they're trying to hold their shit together in the midst of a retrograde.

And it's *so frustrating*, because we always want to be in control, but Mercury itself is way above our paygrade. We can't will our ruling planet back into place and force it to act right, and railing against a retrograde just seems to cause more problems than we're already attempting to juggle.

I spent eight years managing online customer support for a travel website, so Mercury retrogrades were always hellacious on me—I learned to track and anticipate them and brace myself accordingly. But things would still go wrong, and while I normally come across as levelheaded, I have no poker face whatsoever, and the people around me would quickly take notice of my angst.

I was hunched in my cubicle during one particularly rough retrograde, banging my head against my desk and begging my computer to please, *please* act right, when one of my coworkers decided to check in and make sure I was going to survive whatever crisis I was very clearly enduring.

We had the following conversation.

Me: "Mercury went retrograde."

Coworker: "Um, what?"

Me: "Mercury went retrograde. That means it's a bad time for communications and travel."

Coworker: "Huh."

[Beat.]

Coworker: "Wait a minute. *We* work in communications and travel."

Me: "Yep."

Coworker: "So … how bad is it going to be around here?"

Me: "Who knows?"

Coworker: "But it's going to be bad?"

Me: "*Really* bad."

Suddenly apprehensive, my coworker mentioned the retrograde to another coworker, who spread the news to the rest of our team. And then an email went astray, and a witty remark was taken out of context, and traffic inexplicably backed up outside the office. A day later, the entire department was faceplanting into walls and cursing astrology, the only benefit of which being that in the midst of the mayhem, upper management couldn't tell how badly I was screwing up my own projects.

Regardless of the barrage of miscommunications and missed departures, there is an upside to the situation: random, mercurial energy spills into the world when Mercury screeches to a halt and goes stationary, just before it flips the breakers and reverses into its retrograde. And we can use that energy prophylactically.

I'm totally stealing this analogy from Ivo, but picture what happens when you hold a felt-tip pen against a piece of paper. If you move the pen in a line, the ink follows along, but if you keep it in one spot, the ink slowly seeps out in a corona. Mercury does the same thing when it's in a stationary position. So all this unfocused Mercury flotsam is drifting about us, looking for a place to land.

We can harness this detritus and direct it toward spell work, or into any aspect of our lives that needs a hermetic kick. For instance, Mercury retrogrades are a great time to stay home instead of going out and to start working on cleansing and shielding. What are things you might need to communicate in the future? Like, what letters or manuscripts might need to be written three months from now? When Mercury is stationary, we can gather up that extra juice and use it to jumpstart the writing process, knowing that we've gotten ahead, even during a period when our writing would normally be tangled in snags.

During the retrograde itself, we can experiment with magic that flows concurrently along with it. Instead of sending things out into the world, what are things that need to come home? Think about the four corners of the Witches Pyramid: to Know, to Will, to Dare, and to Keep Silent. Willing and Daring might not be the best sides on which to fixate during a Mercury retrograde, but Knowing and Keeping Silent are worth exploring. What can we learn during this time? What secrets need to be kept?

If you're an initiate of an oathbound tradition, now is an excellent time to revisit the oaths you took—are you keeping them effectively? Are there words you said or promises you made during your initiation that need clarification? And if you're not a member of such a tradition, or any tradition, you can still work with this current effectively. Are you dedicated to a particular deity? If so, how is that relationship? Are you upholding your end of any bargain you may have made? What can be done to reinforce that relationship? What reassurances would you like from your deity?

With mundane communication on the fritz, the pathways of spiritual communication can be opened wider. And a beneficial thing we can do on those paths is ask for the ability to set perceived knowledge aside.

This is a technique I picked up a long time ago. The gist is that, in periods of confusion or befuddlement (like, say, a Mercury retrograde), we can ask the gods for their assistance to see the reality of any given situation clearly. For example, on the first night of the retrograde, I might light an orange candle, burn some mercurial incense like benzoin or mace, and chant,

> *Great Hermes, your light in the sky*
> *Fools my eyes and moves backward,*
> *But things are not what they seem.*
> *As above reflects below,*

Help me set aside what I think I know,
So that I may see the truth.

Once I've sent up that initial request, I can recite the prayer anytime during the retrograde when I feel like I'm not understanding a given situation, or whenever I suspect that something is being inadvertently communicated to me. And that takes a lot of the anxiety out of trying to navigate Mercury retrogrades as a Virgo.

I ended up working for a financial advisory firm in the years after I left the travel industry, and my supervisor was a good Christian lady, so superstitions bounced right off her. But I did explain Mercury retrogrades to her anyway, which quickly became an inside joke. Whenever things would go comically awry around the office, one of us would text the other *Retrograde!!!* and then we would giggle and get back to work.

And honestly, laughter is probably the best way to deal with Mercury retrogrades as well. Laughing at the things we can't control takes some of their power away. And in his divine providence, Mercury/Hermes is very much a prankster, so if we can laugh at whatever muck we pratfall into during a retrograde, we can rest easy in the knowledge that

Hermes is laughing too. In fact, he's not laughing at us at all—he is merrily laughing along with us.

Laughter itself is also a good reminder that everything is temporary, astrological splooeyness included. Mercury will eventually go direct, and the internet will mystically start working again, and that friend who stopped speaking to us will realize that they misinterpreted our intentions, and we'll still be around to Virgo it up and laugh at whatever comes next.

At least until Saturn goes retrograde, at which point you should just lock yourself in your house and hide under the couch and eat cookies. I'll join you. Push over and save me some snickerdoodles.

Spell for Honor and Integrity

Ellen Dugan

Virgos are known for their candor and are honest to a fault. Virgos appreciate honesty more than anything else. We are the down-to-earth, shoot-from-the-hip types. Virgos are one of the most critical signs of the zodiac—usually highly critical of ourselves. Yes, we can be blunt, but we are practical and self-aware, and if you want straight-up and honest advice, then ask a Virgo.

So, when I was asked to craft a spell for honor and integrity, I decided to research the root meanings of the words. When you look up synonyms for integrity, the first word that often pops up is *honesty*. Interestingly, *integrity* is classically defined as the quality of being honest and having strong moral principles, and the state of being whole and undivided.

Some folks say that integrity is a firm adherence to a moral code of ethical, artistic, or spiritual values that is followed at all times. Bottom line? Integrity is about doing the right thing even when no one else is watching. That can be a radical concept in a world of virtue signaling, social media, and humblebragging. Integrity and honesty may not be flashy or glamorous, however; people who possess integrity are described as being honest, self-aware, responsible, and truthful. Individuals who exhibit the traits will draw others to them because they are trustworthy and dependable.

In keeping with the practical and down-to-earth qualities of a Virgo, let's work with plant materials that are readily available at this time of the year. This integrity spell also calls on Astrea. She is the Maiden goddess who became the constellation of Virgo.

You will need:

+ White chrysanthemums. Easily grown at home, and these fall bloomers can be gathered from your own garden or picked up for a few bucks from your local florist. In the language of flowers, the white chrysanthemum symbolizes truth.
+ Oak leaves. These represent honor, nobility, and wisdom. Harvest a few leaves only for the spell.
+ Green votive candle and holder

Do not strip the branches of any tree. Likewise, don't decimate a blooming chrysanthemum; a couple of flowers and leaves will do just fine! Arrange your blossoms and leaves on your workspace. Light the candle, take a moment, and center yourself. Lay your fingertips on the plants, and then repeat the spell verse three times.

Astrea, daughter of Zeus and Themis, hear my call,
Help me to always act with integrity to all.
Oak leaves for honor, and spicy white mums for truth,

Combine now in a spell that the Virgos will suit.
May these worthy qualities be drawn to me,
And as I do will it, then so shall it be!

Allow the candle to burn out in a safe place. You may tuck the floral components in a vase and enjoy them for a few days. After they fade, add them to the compost or yard waste bin. Blessed be, my fellow Virgo witches!

A BRIEF BIO OF RAYMOND BUCKLAND

* * *

Katrina Rasbold

Born in London on August 31, 1934, to an English mother and Romanichal father, Raymond Buckland exemplifies the Virgoan witch with a lifetime of creating, organizing, and adapting. At the age of twelve, his uncle, George, introduced him to Spiritualism, igniting an enduring passion for the occult. In 1955, he married Rosemary Moss and the couple moved to Brentwood, Long Island, New York, in 1962.

Two books, *The Witch-Cult in Western Europe* by Margaret A. Murray (1921) and *Witchcraft Today* (1954) by Gerald Gardner, at last gave a name and structure to his spiritual leanings. Buckland established a relationship with Gardner via letters and telephone calls that lasted until Gardner's death in 1964.

In 1963, the Bucklands flew to Scotland to be initiated by Monique Wilson (Lady Olwen), one of Gardner's High Priestesses. Gardner was present for the initiation, and this would be the only time Buckland and Gardner met in person as Gardner died soon afterward.

Gardnerian Witchcraft came to the United States when the Bucklands started the New York Coven. Initially, they followed the tradition of secrecy around both their practice and their identity as witches; however, a journalist named Lisa Hoffman named him as the group leader. To his benefit and detriment, Buckland quickly became known as an authority on witchcraft.

After Raymond and Rosemary Buckland divorced in 1974, he penned *The Tree: A Complete Book of Saxon Witchcraft*, a book reflecting his drift away from Gardnerian Craft. He presented Seax Wicca, a new tradition that emerged from his developing experience with Wicca. This path did not carry forward the degree system used by Gardner and was democratic rather than authoritarian. His correspondence course on Seax Wicca included over a thousand students.

Over five decades, Buckland wrote an impressive number of books, including some of the most seminal volumes on witchcraft, plus a significant amount of fiction penned under the name Tony Earll (an antigram of Not Really). His 1986 publication of *The Complete Book of Witchcraft*, also known as The Big Blue Book, quickly became the consummate resource on witchcraft and Wicca.

Buckland amassed significant witchcraft-related artifacts throughout his life, which he shared with the public by opening a museum. Over the years, this collection and the museum moved through various locations and curators, either on display or in storage. The full museum collection was briefly reestablished in New Orleans in 1999 where it faltered before being saved by Rev. Velvet Reith. Some parts of the collection were damaged, and some pieces were lost. Velvet went to great lengths to prevent the collection from suffering any additional deterioration. Ultimately, Buckland's precious relics landed in the hands of Kat Tigner and Toni Rotonda, owners of The Cat and The Cauldron in Columbus, Ohio. This collection is currently on display at the Buckland Museum of Witchcraft and Magick in Cleveland, Ohio, and curated by Steven Intermill.

Although Buckland officially retired from public Paganism in 1992, he continued writing and making appearances at festivals with other pioneers of Paganism for many years. He remained in relative seclusion until his death in 2017 from pneumonia-related heart and lung problems.

A Sampling of Virgo Occultists

PAUL VINCENT BEYERL
master herbalist, author, and Wiccan Priest
(September 2, 1945)

ALISON HARLOW
Feri tradition witch, feminist, and activist
(August 29, 1934)

MURRY HOPE
occultist, priestess, and author
(September 17, 1929)

PAUL HUSON
artist, author, screenwriter, and occultist
(September 19, 1942)

MARIE CATHERINE LAVEAU
Voodoo Queen of New Orleans
(September 10, 1801)

SILVER RAVENWOLF
bestselling author and witch elder
(September 11, 1956)

GWEN THOMPSON
founder of New England Covens
of Traditionalist Witches
(September 16, 1928)

THE SWAY OF YOUR MOON SIGN

Ivo Dominguez, Jr.

The Moon is the reservoir of your emotions, thoughts, and all your experiences. The Moon guides your subconscious, your unconscious, and your instinctive response in the moment. The Moon serves as the author, narrator, and the musical score in the ongoing movie in your mind that summarizes and mythologizes your story. The Moon is like a scrying mirror, a sacred well, that gives answers to the question of the meaning of your life. The style and the perspective of your Moon sign shapes your story, a story that starts as a reflection of your Sun sign's impetus. The remembrance of your life events is a condensed subjective story, and it is your Moon sign that summarizes and categorizes the data stream of your life.

In witchcraft, the Moon is our connection and guide to the physical and energetic tides in nature, the astral plane, and other realities. The Moon in the heavens as it moves through signs and phases also pulls and pushes on your aura. The Moon in your birth chart reveals the intrinsic qualities and patterns in your aura, which affects the form your magick takes. Your Sun sign may be the source of your essence and power, but your Moon sign shows how you use that power in your magick. This chapter describes the twelve possible arrangements of Moon signs with a Virgo Sun and what each combination yields.

Moon in Aries

Careful. Virgo does not easily pair with impulsive Aries. However, when you find the right blend of the two, you can go far. An Aries Moon gives you the appearance of confidence and the dynamism that marks a natural leader. A Virgo Sun can make sure that your enthusiastically presented ideas are backed up with details and plans. When these two sides of your nature fall out of sync, you underperform and may criticize yourself and/or disappoint others. This Aries is nearly feral, not a team player, and needs to be controlled by your Virgo Sun. This combination makes you want to take charge of most situations whenever possible. You really can do a marvelous job when you manage yourself as much as you do the situation.

You are more passionate than most Virgos, but you tend to be leerier of the softer emotions. Try to give people who are gushing sweetness and positivity a chance; some of them are authentic. If you need an incentive, the more you get in touch with your emotions, the more you'll understand what motivates people. This will make you more effective in the world. You'll also have an easier time finding partners who are good for you. You don't like being bored and your idea of recreation does not include much in the way of rest. Like most Virgos, your nerves can get too keyed up. Find things that consistently relax and soothe you when you are overwrought and use them. You are not inclined to be a social butterfly, and you wouldn't enjoy being one. However, you will be happier and healthier if you cultivate a social circle to give you support and advice you'll trust.

An Aries Moon, like all the fire element Moons, easily stretches forth to connect with the energy of other beings. Your fiery qualities act to cleanse and protect your aura from picking up other people's emotional debris or being influenced by your environment. It is relatively easy for you to blend your energy with others and to separate cleanly. However, take care not to use up too much of your own energy or exhaust yourself. Learning to sense your flow and to moderate it is essential. The energy field and magick of an Aries Moon tends to move and change faster than any other sign, but it is harder to hold to a specific task or shape. This can be overcome with self-awareness and practice.

Moon in Taurus

Both your Sun and Moon are in the element of earth, which gives you a grounded and resolute nature. This combination tends to offer luck in worldly affairs and a good understanding of how to get things done. Despite these gifts, you tend not to be highly ambitious unless you are providing for someone else. Scarcity or concerns for stability can nag at you and wear you down. Have faith in your capacity to get what you need, and though you have perseverance, the most important quality you need to develop is patience. You tend to be nostalgic, retro, or conservative in your tastes for yourself. However, you attract many different types of friends and colleagues because of your loyal and straightforward nature. When you say you are a friend, you truly mean it.

This Moon encourages you to stop and smell the roses, to enjoy the world. Allow yourself to revel in your Moon's Taurean sensuality. In astrology, the Moon is said to be exalted in Taurus, which means that it favors success. For a Virgo, this combination also gives you some creativity in the arts and practical matters. You have an innate sense of how to look at a project and break it into bite-sized chunks so that it can be accomplished. Just try to be more open to last-minute changes in plans. This combination tends to experience more fear of missing out as the years go by. Creating experiences that you can share with others is the best medicine for you when you are feeling stuck in your life. Procrastination is a big warning sign that you need to recharge your connection to the things that bring you joy and purpose.

A Taurus Moon generates an aura that is magnetic and pulls energy inward. You are good at raising energy for yourself and others in workings and rituals. This Moon also makes it easier to create strong shields and wards. If something does manage to breach your shields or create some other type of energetic injury, get some healing help. Generally, people with a Taurus Moon have less flexibility in their aura. You can work toward improving your flexibility, but the quick fix is to create new boundaries or a larger container. Astral travel and other forms of soul travel are harder to begin with this Moon sign, so draw upon your Virgo mutable earth to become more flexible. However, once in motion, it is a stronger version of you that travels and often exceeds what many witches can do.

♊
Moon in Gemini

This combination is a double dose of Mercury rulership, which means you are brilliant, perceptive, and inventive. Your Virgo Sun is always telling your Gemini Moon to dig deeper, so you truly are an eternal student. Over time you will become competent in many things and can be an expert when you apply yourself. This combination gives you many career and interest options. You'd be good as a researcher, a salesperson, a healthcare provider, an IT person, and so on. One area that may need more investigation is your heart. It is often easier for you to know what you think about someone than what you feel about them. You are good at looking calm and poised, so don't worry about being found out on whatever you are holding back until you are ready to talk. Gemini gives you more adaptability than most Virgos, so you can chameleon yourself into many social or work settings.

Cultivating patience is essential, not just for your projects, but also for how you deal with others. You are really good at rationalizing things to manage discomforts, but some type of meditation or relaxation process would be helpful. This combination has a tendency to live too much in their head. Find the time to be outdoors in nature as this will make you more grounded. Your to-do list for your life is long, and giving more attention to your body and health will make it possible to check more items off the list. Your Virgo Sun is health focused, but your Gemini Moon is not.

A Gemini Moon, like all the air Moons, makes it easier to engage in soul travel and psychism and gives the aura greater flexibility. You have a quicksilver aura that seeks connection but not a merger with other beings and energies. When an air type aura reaches out and touches something, it can quickly read and copy the patterns it finds. A Gemini Moon gives the capacity to quickly adapt and respond to changing energy conditions in working magick or using the psychic senses. However, turbulent spiritual atmospheres are felt strongly and can be uncomfortable or cause harm. A wind can pick up and carry dust and debris, and the same is true for an aura. If you need to cleanse your energy, become still, and the debris will simply fall out of your aura.

Moon in Cancer

A Cancer Moon means you are more in touch with your feelings than most Virgos. You also have a need for a close circle of family or friends to feel secure in your life. You are empathetic and practical in your approach to matters of the heart. The Cancer Moon gives you a desire to protect and take care of those you like or love. Your Virgo Sun is also good at coming up with reasons why that is a good idea. This combination can produce a consciousness that joins emotional intelligence with rational thought to produce wisdom and shrewd choices. It can also use emotion and thought to avoid a reasonable approximation of reality. When you use the best of Virgo and Cancer, you are amazing, excel at living, and a gift to those around you.

Both Virgo and Cancer are prone to be sensitive when it comes to criticism. Your sense of being hurt can be triggered into a feedback loop. Be mindful of this so you can interrupt a pattern that is hurtful and unproductive. Often you do come up with the best plans and ideas, but you may have to explain them more than one way so they are understood. Take a breath and take a different approach to avoid some distress. You may have delicate digestion or some other physical indicator for when you are stressed. Your feelings turn into physical sensations easily. Turn this to your advantage by heeding the warning early and taking care of yourself. This will let you live a longer and healthier life.

A Cancer Moon, like all the water Moons, gives the aura a magnetic pull that wants to merge with whatever is nearby. Imagine two drops of water growing closer until they barely touch and how they pull together to become one larger drop. The aura of a person with a Cancer Moon is more likely to retain the patterns and energies it touches. This can be a good thing or a problem depending on what is absorbed. You must take extra care to cleanse and purify yourself before and after magickal work whenever possible. One of the gifts that comes with this Moon is a capacity for healing touch that offers comfort while filling in and healing disruptions in other people's energy.

Moon in Leo

This fiery Moon makes for a bighearted, exuberant, and self-assured version of Virgo. There is a great deal of kindness and polite charm as well. This Moon increases your optimism and hopefulness so that you recover from setbacks more quickly than the average Virgo. This combination tends to produce people who are high-minded and principled. You tend to be more trusting as you expect the best of people, though in time you may swing to being more distrustful than most as a result of bad experiences. When this happens, you can be dramatic in a way that gives even Leo Suns a run for their money. You give a lot to your beloveds, and you expect the same in return. Your Virgo nature will always notice what can be improved in your relationships, and your Leo Moon will present your insights in an unmistakable fashion. Take a breath and reevaluate the best way to say what you need to be effective and gentle.

When it comes to projects that you undertake and your workplace, you tend to do best when you have the authority to do as you see fit. Your Leo Moon expects the good work that you are doing to be recognized and rewarded. Unfortunately, that is not the way it usually works. Also, your Virgo Sun inhibits you from displaying your exemplary work. You'll do better in the world if you develop the habit of publicizing what you do. Don't hide your light and point it out when you shine. Ask for what you need and deserve.

A Leo Moon, like all the fire element Moons, easily stretches forth to connect with the energy of other beings. The fiery qualities cleanse and protect your aura from picking up other people's emotional debris or being influenced by your environment. It is relatively easy for you to blend your energy with others and to separate cleanly. The Leo Moon also makes it easier for you to find your center and stay centered. The fixed fire of Leo makes it easier to hold large amounts of energy that can be applied for individual and collective workings. You are particularly well suited to ritual leadership or being the primary shaper of energy in a working. Combined with your Virgo Sun, this Moon grants special insights in spotting what is off and fixing it in spells, rituals, and healing work.

Moon in Virgo

Being a double Virgo produces a great focus on all matters of the mind. You love to think, study, analyze, and have clear opinions on what is right or wrong. Internally, you are reviewing and rating everything in the world around you. For the sake of peace, you are cautious about sharing opinions. This is usually the right choice, but be sure you say your piece when you must. Otherwise, some of that energy may turn to unnecessary self-criticism. You know it is time to speak up and speak out when you have lined up all the details and have worked through all the angles logically. Any career that makes use of your intellect, such as journalism, writing, teaching, library science, researching, and so on, feeds your soul. Though you are often good in leadership or management roles, you can find them to be tiresome and often less rewarding. Be mindful that your gaze can feel like a laser beam when you are examining someone.

Though you gain much of your satisfaction in life from the work you do, you do need a few people you can count on. You tend not to be initially romantic, but you are loyal and drawn to interesting people. Intelligence, talent, and accomplishments are the spice of life for you. Although you look stern or unassailable most of the time, you are acutely sensitive to criticism. You have a very refined sense of aesthetics that you apply to your clothing, décor, music, and all parts of your life. This arises from a feeling of comfort that comes from orderliness and harmony. This contributes to your urges to do work that improves you and the world. Resist the urge to throw your hands in the air and walk away when you see the state the world is in.

A Virgo Moon, like all the earth element Moons, generates an aura that is magnetic and pulls energy inward. This Moon also makes it easier to create strong thoughtforms and energy constructs. Virgo

Moons are best at perceiving and understanding patterns and process in auras, energy, spells, and so on. You can be quite good at spotting what is off and finding a way to remedy the situation. This gives the potential to do healing work and curse breaking among other things. The doubled mutability of Virgo Sun and Moon makes it easier to shape-shift and to cast illusions and glamours upon yourself.

♎

Moon in Libra

You have a keen capacity for finding joy and beauty in life. You are more socially minded than most Virgos. You know how to be a friend and how to show that you care. Your positive stance on the world is not always realistic, more aspirational, but this allows you to better the world by trying to make the ideal into the real. People are attracted to you and charmed by you, even though you are fairly quiet and aren't trying to draw attention. You generally have a live and let live attitude, though internally you do keep track of people's actions. You avoid or sidestep people or things that offend your taste or ethics.

You are self-sufficient, professional, and diplomatic, so most people do not notice the distance you keep from them. If it is about work or a task that must be done, you will find a way to make it work.

You are selective in who you bring into your life. For you, romance and friendships often begin through mental pursuits, or a shared love of specific types of art, music, media, and so on. You also are more comfortable having people close who have orderly and stable lives. You give off a dignified air that can be confused with being aloof. Make sure that you let people know how you feel. Your Libra Moon craves a harmonious environment, and your Virgo Sun helps manage your life to fill those needs. Reciprocity and a balance of give-and-take is important to you in all settings, both personal and professional. This may lead to an interest in the law, politics, sociology, or social justice.

A Libra Moon, like all the air Moons, makes it easier to engage in soul travel and psychism and gives the aura greater flexibility. When you are working well with your Libra Moon, you can make yourself a neutral and clear channel for information from spirits and other entities. You are also able to tune in to unspoken requests when doing divinatory work. The auras of people with Libra Moon are very capable at bridging and equalizing differences between the subtle bodies of groups of people. This allows you to bring order and harmony to energies raised and shaped in a group ritual. You may have a talent for bargaining with spirits and placating or smoothing over disturbances.

Moon in Scorpio

This makes for an intensely passionate nature with a desire to take on the world. This is an assertive combination that appears icy and in control on the surface but is stormy underneath. The Scorpio Moon puts up a wall around you so that you need to make a choice to laugh and let people see your lighter side. Otherwise, people will peg you as serious, mysterious, and unapproachable. One of your challenges is to find the proper balance between your head and your heart. Try to let your head lead more because, though your intuition is often right, the accuracy of your emotional reactions is hit-or-miss. You have a sharp intellect that catches every detail, and you are precise and methodical. You think of yourself as highly rational, and this is half true. You are gifted but will do better when you try to be more objective. Also, winning an argument with logic and carefully chosen phrases doesn't always lead to a rewarding outcome. Consider the relationships at play and whether or not they would be harmed. Let your friends and loved ones into your thought process as they do have insights that would be useful. Moreover, your natural tendency is to keep too many secrets. In general, you do not share enough, which can lead to confusion or heartache.

You have a strong survival instinct, which means that sometimes you will put your principles aside and choose pragmatism. This can also lead you to be protective of the ones you care for. Make sure that your level of protectiveness is comfortable for those around you. Personal autonomy matters to you, so just consider how you would feel in their shoes.

A Scorpio Moon, like all the water Moons, gives the aura a magnetic pull that wants to merge with whatever is nearby. You easily absorb information about other people, spirits, places, and so on. If you are not careful, the information and the emotions will loop and repeat in your mind. To release what you have picked up, acknowledge what you perceive and then reframe its meaning in your own words. The energy and magick of a Scorpio Moon are adept at probing and moving past barriers, shields, and wards. This also gives you the power to remove things that should not be present. This combination makes it easier for you to imbue objects with power, spell work, or consecrations.

Moon in Sagittarius

You have an abundance of enthusiasm, optimism, and the energy to pursue your dreams and interests. You are outspoken and would have a hard time bottling up your thoughts or feelings.

Your fiery Moon and your earthy Sun are very different from each other, and the range of attitudes and behaviors you express is very wide. However, both are mutable, so there is a sympathy and grace between them that helps synchronize the gifts each brings. You have a great deal more natural charisma than most Virgos and an excellent sense of humor. You can have the capacity to develop strong people skills and technical skills. You would do well in leadership or managerial roles. Some with this combination enjoy performing in front of people if they lean into their Sagittarius Moon. This blend can also lead toward humanitarian and environmental work as Sagittarius inspires work for the community and Virgo is pragmatic.

You are highly adaptable and quick-witted, so even if you drop the ball occasionally, you'll pick it up and recover. Sometimes that Moon gets you stuck so deep in philosophical thought that it turns into procrastination. You are healthier and happier when you are busy. Boredom caused by a lack of useful or exciting things to do is kryptonite to you. This is just as bad for your health as stress, and in some ways it's worse. Travel, even if it is only a day trip or an afternoon outing, will do you a great deal of good. You do have a need for freedom and a desire to explore new territories. This applies to all parts of your life, inner and outer. You tend to be happier with friends and loved ones who give you space and love to work and/or adventure with you.

The auras of people with Sagittarius Moon are the most adaptable of the fire Moons. Your energy can reach far and change its shape easily. You are particularly good at affecting other people's energy or the energy of a place. Like the other fire Moons, your aura is good at cleansing itself, but it is not automatic and requires your conscious choice. The mutable fire of Sagittarius is changeable and can go from a small ember to a pillar of fire that reaches the sky. It is important that you manage your energy so it is somewhere between the extremes of almost out and furious inferno. This aura has star power when you light it up, and physical and nonphysical beings will look and listen.

Moon in Capricorn

Capricorn Moon with Virgo Sun joins together two of the hardest working signs. Double the earth and more momentum to get things done no matter what is in your way. You have a strong sense of purpose and enough self-discipline to tackle almost anything. You are more serious and self-sufficient than most Virgo Sun people. Much of your success comes from the planning, plotting, and analysis that a Capricorn Moon loves. You have amazing stamina and resilience and a powerful mind. The downside to this gift is that you can be too serious, and your Virgo Sun will worry even more. Schedule time for recreation or it won't happen often enough. You also are prone to being too harsh a critic of your own efforts. Cut yourself some slack and you'll improve faster. You pride yourself on your poise and self-control, but if you don't relax enough, you will erupt in a memorable way.

Your personal standards apply to you and not to others. This combination produces a smaller tolerance level for listening to complaints or kvetching or signs of giving up. You'll have fewer unnecessary conflicts when you understand people on their own terms. If you do need something to change, try persuasion first rather than transforming your magnetic charm into a coercion. Make it a practice to strengthen your compassion and patience for others. At home, you need a partner who can go toe to toe with you. They need to have their own accomplishments and projects so that you can bond over strategizing. Mutual support and reciprocity are essential to happiness in your relationships. You are not generally romantic, but you love deeply and are truly loyal. Create a home and a family of choice that suits you, not what society tries to enforce.

A Capricorn Moon, like all the earth element Moons, generates an aura that is magnetic and pulls energy inward. What you draw to yourself tends to stick and solidify, so be wary, especially when doing healing work or cleansings. The magick of a Capricorn Moon is excellent at imposing a pattern or creating a container in a working. Your spells and workings tend to be durable. You also have a knack for building wards and doing protective magick. You have a gift for banishing negative energies and entities. With proper training, you are good at manifesting the things you need.

Moon in Aquarius

This combination produces an inventive, resourceful, and lively mind. In addition to a powerful intellect, you also have strong intuition that counterbalances your thought process. You tend to examine your own life, feelings, and motivations more than most Virgos. Your imagination is formidable, and if you can create it in your mind, you can find a way to make it happen in the world. You have an aptitude for finding the steps that transform an idea into a reality. Aquarius makes you more idealistic and ideological than most Virgos. People tend to see you as less conventional and more experimental, even when you are trying to look conventional. You are an imaginative and a rational thinker. You are a good storyteller, and stories often work better than rhetoric to make your point. Take care that you pick the right time, place, and audience so that you will inspire people rather than rub them the wrong way. You know how to project confident and calm assurance. You'd do well as a teacher, healer, counselor, coach, or in any situation that calls for imparting knowledge and helping people become better.

Make sure you find partners and close friends who can keep up or learn to look back and check on them. For you, candor and precise communications are essential for solid relationships. You do love debating everything. Additionally, please remind yourself that people need to specifically and explicitly hear from you that you care about them. Whether it is at home or in the world, you can be a source of stability in chaotic times. When you are in survival mode or laser focused on a project, you may be a little too cold, too detached, so you need to choose to turn up your warmth.

Like all the air Moons, the Aquarius Moon encourages a highly mobile and flexible aura. Without a strong focus, the power of an air subtle body becomes scattered and diffuse. If you have an air Moon, an emphasis should be placed on finding and focusing on your center of energy. Grounding is important, but focusing on your core and center is more important. From that center, you can strengthen and stabilize your power. People with

Aquarius Moon are good at shaping and holding a specific thoughtform or energy pattern and transferring it to other people or into objects. Your Virgo energy allows you to use this Moon for more precise divination.

Moon in Pisces

You are grounded in the world by Virgo and yet also leave it regularly through the mystic power of a Pisces Moon. You need to guard your heart because you feel deeply and notice all the details and flaws of the world. You are equally hurt by thoughtless actions or intentional cruelty to you or to others. Thicken your skin and put up some shields, but don't harden your beautiful heart. You may also want to pull back and become disengaged from the people and things around you when it seems too much. You would like the world to be more honorable and straightforward than it is. Occasionally you do need a personal quest, a journey, or perhaps just a regular yoga or meditation session to refresh yourself so you can return to your work. Gazing at the ocean, a river, or any water feature is good for you.

You have an abundance of imagination and deep wellsprings of creativity that can be applied in the arts, the sciences, or in business. If you don't have enough opportunity for self-expression, or block the flow, it can turn into fretting and brooding. You like to please people, which can lead to saying yes when you have no time to finish what you've already begun. You attract people who are in need of your compassion and a friendly ear. This is part of your work, but know when to take a break. When you lose your balance, this combo creates a tendency toward pessimism and nit-picking. Your physical health also relies on keeping yourself in equilibrium. In matters of the heart, you are very giving, and when you love someone, you overlook their flaws. You'd do better with a partner who is at least as far along in their development as you are.

With a Pisces Moon, the emphasis should be on learning to feel and control the rhythm of your energetic motion in your aura. Water Moon sign auras are flexible, cohesive, and magnetic, so they tend to ripple and rock like waves. Pisces Moon is the most likely to pick up and hang on to unwanted emotions or energies. Be careful, develop good shielding practices, and make cleansing yourself and your home a regular practice. Pisces Moon people are the best at energizing, comforting, and healing disruptions in other people's auras. Your Virgo energy lets you use this Moon to find the best possible futures out of the many possibilities.

TAROT
CORRESPONDENCES

♍

You can use the tarot cards in your work as a Virgo witch for more than divination. They can be used as focal points in meditations and trance to connect with the power of your sign or element or to understand them more fully. They are great on your altar as an anchor for the powers you are calling. You can use the Minor Arcana cards to tap into Sun, Venus, or Mercury in Virgo energy even when they are in other signs in the heavens. If you take a picture of a card, shrink the image and print it out; you can fold it up and place it in spell bags or jars as an ingredient.

Virgo Major Arcana

The Hermit

All the Earth Signs

The Ace of Pentacles

Virgo Minor Arcana

8 of Pentacles	Sun in Virgo
9 of Pentacles	Venus in Virgo
10 of Pentacles	Mercury in Virgo

Thumper Forge

I started practicing witchcraft in my late teens, and I reluctantly accepted how big of a Virgo I really am in my early twenties. But it wasn't until I was deep in the woods, with gunshots in the distance and everyone around me baying at the Moon, that I fully embraced my identity as a Virgo witch.

It was not exactly what I'd envisioned when I got invited to a Pagan campout for men who love men. But looking back, I'm glad I attended, if only to prevent all the carnage that would've inevitably erupted had there not been a Virgo witch present to ruin the evening for everyone else.

I should probably start at the beginning.

The campground itself was nestled in the wilds of South-Central Texas, far enough out in the country so that we could genuinely commune with nature, but not so far that we couldn't make it to a Walmart in under twenty minutes. And gay men are nothing if not plagued with ingenuity, so while the other campsites on the land had nothing more than firepits, ours featured a hot water shower and an aboveground pool.

There wasn't much of an agenda for the weekend—it was just supposed to be a bonding experience, and an excuse to run about the forest wearing sarongs and stompy boots—but one of the organizers had announced that there would be a Wild Hunt ritual on Saturday night, and while participation wasn't exactly mandatory, it was understood that all of us in attendance would at the very least show up.

I should add here that the organizer and I worked with very different definitions of the word *ritual*: I tended to think about ritual in terms of semiformal, singular, or group actions designed to accomplish a spiritual or magical goal, where he was more like, "We can get away with a lot of giggly-naughty stuff without repercussion if we call whatever it is we're doing a ritual, like the good Pagans we are."

And yeah, I know how uncharitable that sounds. But I'd also been trained to view ritual in terms of results, not as a rationalization for festival sex. Not that I have anything against festival sex, mind you; I just think we're better off calling it what it is rather than trying to frame it as a religious indulgence.

Anyway, after a day and a half of lounging and frolicking, it was time to prepare for the Wild Hunt. We gathered around the organizer, who was dramatically backlit by the setting Sun, to find out what we were in for. And as he explained the details, my urge to trade my sarong back in for office casual hit a new high.

Attendees were instructed to divide into two groups: one group would be the Hounds, and the other would be the Stags. Once the ritual began, the Stags would run off and hide in the woods, and after a few minutes, the Hounds would bound into the woods in pursuit. And if a Hound found a Stag, the Stag was required to do... *anything* the Hound wanted.

"Some of you remember this ritual from our last campout," the organizer said, and a couple of the guys leered in response. "It's *very* powerful, and we're going to raise a *lot* of energy."

So here was my problem with that: raising energy is only one part of an effective ritual. Once the energy is raised, it needs to be put to use, directed into a purpose or a working. Raising energy and just letting it sit there is, at best, an exercise in futility, and at worst, a recipe for disaster. But in this case, raising energy *was* the purpose—nobody had thought through as to where all that energy was supposed to go once the ritual ended.

And, of course, then there were the gunshots.

A small ranch abutted the campground, the conservative owners of which were not amused about having godless heathens as their next-door neighbors. And so, whenever the Pagans showed up en masse, the ranchers would stand near the property line and fire guns into the air. There hadn't been, as far as I knew, any actual confrontations, but we were all very careful not to accidentally cross onto the ranch's land, since the maxim "Trespassers will be shot; survivors will be shot again" was pretty much the word of the law in those parts.

"Hound or Stag?"

"Pardon me?" I asked, popping out of my anxiety-induced ruminations.

"Are you a Hound or a Stag?" the organizer asked again.

"Oh. Um … I'm a drummer," I replied. And I scurried over to stand with the three other men who were feeling neither canine nor cervine.

Within a few moments, everyone else decided on the animal persona they would assume and lined up across from each other, like they were gearing up for a decidedly NC-17 round of Red Rover. The organizer stood between the two lines and began leading a meditation to help the participants get into character.

"Stags, feel your antlers," he intoned, as a rifle cracked somewhere in the background. "Feel your hooves. Feel your hides. Hounds, feel your fur. Feel your claws. Feel your fangs."

At some point, it dawned on the drummers that we were supposed to be Doing Something, so we grabbed whatever percussion instruments we could find and, after a few false starts, settled on a beat. The Hounds and Stags continued to feel themselves, and, quite to my surprise, energy began to build.

Night had fallen by this point, and the Hounds were starting to sniff the air and growl, while the Stags were huffing and stamping at the ground nervously. The drummers had found an almost-but-not-quite trance-inducing rhythm; everyone was really getting into character, much more than my cynical self assumed they would.

And then two things happened: The various dogs that people had brought with them for the weekend trotted over, sat down in front of the Hounds, and stared at the Stags intently. And another gunshot rang out from the next property. Right as the organizer yelled, "RUN, STAGS. RUN TO THE WOODS."

The Stags took off and quickly disappeared into the dark brush. And as the Hounds started howling and tensed to sprint after them, I handed my drum to the guy next to me and scampered to my tent.

I can't give you a good reason for why I'd packed a Sharpie, other than I'm a Virgo, and I'd figured it might come in handy. I also pulled a notepad out of my bag that I'd meant to use for journaling, then headed over to the currently unsupervised campfire to kitbash a ritual of my own.

Like I said, energy had definitely been raised, but it didn't feel sensual, or even lascivious; it felt like a Hunt. And there were guys in the woods pretending to be deer, with actual dogs possibly confusing them for actual prey, and, within spitting distance, a posse of grumpy ranchers with automatic weapons and boundary issues. If left unchecked, the Hunt energy would find somewhere to go, and as far as I was concerned, the night's festivities could easily reach a grisly ending.

Clearly, it was up to me to save everyone, because when was it not? Standing at the edge of the campfire, I let myself kind of meld with the energy, and when I felt like I had its attention, I started scribbling out petitions and tossing them into the flames.

I don't remember what I wrote—I think it was mainly general requests for good fortune and prosperity. But every time one of the pages caught fire, a little bit of the energy went with it. Before long, the air around me lost the tinge of a potential bloodbath, so I took a moment to ground, gathered my things, and trotted back over to the drummers, who'd really gotten into their jobs and hadn't even noticed I'd left.

Shortly thereafter, the Hounds and Stags started emerging from the woods and wandering back to camp. A couple of the Stags had been caught, but their captor Hounds didn't really ask too much of them—some smooches and consensual gropes, but nothing that would require therapy back in the Real World. Most of the guys were like, "Well, that was fun," although the ones who had participated in a Wild Hunt at the last campout expressed some disappointment.

"It was like the energy was different this time," one guy remarked, eliciting nods from the others.

The organizer kind of leapt at that and launched into a whole explanation of how "energy is so unpredictable" and "we just never know what's going to happen when we raise such powerful energy," and I managed to cover my eyeroll by pretending to stifle a yawn.

"Wow, I sure am tired all of a sudden," I said. "I'm probably going to turn in soon."

The organizer gave me a sympathetic smile. "That's understandable," he said. "All that drumming raised a *lot* of energy."

I never told anyone about the work I did during the Wild Hunt (and if any of those guys are reading this, sorry, y'all; it was totally my fault), because I didn't do it for praise, or to show off what an amazing witch I was. I did it, because in any situation where things start to go off course, a Virgo will jump in to steer things back toward safer ground. If only because we spend our free time analyzing everything that could go wrong and plotting out contingency plans.

I was already a witch going into the weekend, but I was undeniably a Virgo witch by the end of it. And because of this experience, if anyone ever springs another Wild Hunt on me, I'll be like, "Wow, sounds great! I actually brought a ritual script with me, just in case. Now, who wants to be in charge of directing the energy?"

YOUR RISING SIGN'S INFLUENCE

Ivo Dominguez, Jr.

The rising sign, also known as the ascendant, is the sign that was rising on the eastern horizon at the time and place of your birth. In the birth chart, it is on the left side of the chart on the horizontal line that divides the upper and lower halves of the chart. Your rising sign is also the cusp of your first house. It is often said that the rising sign is the mask you wear to the world, but it is much more than that. It is also the portal through which you experience the world. The sign of your ascendant colors and filters those experiences. Additionally, when people first meet you, they meet your rising sign. This means that they interact with you based on their perception of that sign rather than your Sun sign. This in turn has an impact on you and how you view yourself. As they get to know you over time, they'll meet you as your Sun sign. Your ascendant is like the colorful clouds that hide the Sun at dawn, and as the Sun continues to rise, it is revealed.

The rising sign will also have an influence on your physical appearance as well as your style of dress. To some degree, your voice, mannerisms, facial expressions, stance, and gait are also swayed by the sign of your ascendant. The building blocks of your public persona come from your rising sign. How you arrange those building blocks is guided by your Sun sign, but your Sun sign must work with what it has been given. For witches, the rising sign shows some of the qualities and foundations for the magickal personality you can construct. The magickal personality is much more than simply the shifting into the right headspace, collecting ritual gear, the lighting of candles, and so on. The magickal persona is a construct that is developed through your magickal and spiritual practices to serve as an interface between different parts of the self. The magickal persona, also known as the magickal personality, can also act as a container or boundary so that the mundane and the magickal parts of a person's life can each have its own space. Your rising also gives clues about which magickal techniques will come naturally to you. This chapter describes the twelve possible arrangements of rising signs with a Virgo Sun and what each combination produces. There are 144 possible kinds of Virgo when you take into consideration the Moon signs and rising signs. You may wish to reread the chapter on your Moon sign after reading about your rising sign so you can better understand these influences when they are merged.

Aries Rising

The earth of Virgo blends with an Aries rising to push you to be driven, exuberant, and brave. Mostly this is a good thing, but a bit of caution and reconnaissance before you leap into something would be wise. This is a forceful combo with high aspirations and tons of energy, but you need to be careful not to burn out. You may not run out of energy, but you will get too crispy around the edges from this fire if you don't learn to rein yourself in. You are more fitness focused and physically active than most Virgos. Be cautious that you don't overindulge in life's physical pleasures because you are drawn to excess.

Having the ruling planets of Mercury and Mars means you will radiate charismatic energy, or at the very least friendly energy that will attract people's attention. This will wax and wane in intensity but is always present. Learn to give small warnings so that people know when to give you space. You want to inspire and lead people, and that will be harder if you seem erratic. You do better when you have trusted friends and companions. They need to know that you care about them, and your words and actions must demonstrate your affection.

An Aries rising means that when you reach out to draw in power, fire will answer faster and more intensely. Use your Virgo mutability to shape the fire you call. When working with air or water, use your rising to tune in to air and your Sun to tune in to water. This combination makes it easier for you to summon and call forth spirits and powers and create bindings. The creation of servitors, amulets, and charms is favored as well. This rising also amplifies protective magick for yourself and others.

Taurus Rising

A Taurus rising can bring serenity and steadfast determination that complements Virgo's analytical nature. If you are not vigilant, this can also turn into unreasonable stubbornness and rigidity. Ask yourself whether you are acting with kindness and compassion. Listen to the people you trust when they make observations or give advice. You have a greater need for quiet times and a cozy home than most Virgos. Investing in clothing that is comfortable and fits you well is important as it acts as protection as you go about your activities in the world. You love beautiful things, and this love leads to beautiful clutter. Try to declutter by giving things away as Virgos do better in orderly spaces.

You have good instincts for helping people discover their innate talents. You also know how to put people at ease. You would do well working with plants or the natural sciences, as a chef, or as anything else that is anchored in the physical world. It is easier for you to talk about other people's emotions, but you are shy when it comes to expressing yours.

Working with people teaches you how to show your heart. As you get older, try to maintain or increase your level of physical activity to lift up your vitality and to keep your body comfortable.

Taurus rising strengthens your aura and the capacity to maintain a more solid shape to your energy. This gives you stronger shields and allows you to create thoughtforms and spells that are longer lasting. This combination makes it a bit harder to call energy, but once it is started, the flow is strong. You have a powerful gift for invocations, trance work, and hypnosis. This combo also makes it easier to work with nature spirits and plant spirits.

♊

Gemini Rising

This rising sharpens your Virgo communication skills and makes you a compelling writer or speaker. You are more inquisitive about everything and everyone than most Virgos. You are likely to be a lifelong learner and may shift careers several times. You'd get closer to achieving your goals if you dug deeper into the details and focused on sticking to your plans. Asking others for their ideas is good, but doing your own research is better. To relax, try knitting, painting, carving, playing a musical instrument, juggling, or anything that uses your hands in a skillful way. These sorts of activities greatly reduce stress and improve mental focus.

You come across as bright, sometimes edgy, and genuinely interested in the people around you. You tend to treat your friends as if they were family and your family as if they were friends. Usually this works, but when it doesn't, quickly adjust how you see and treat the person who doesn't like this arrangement. Your emotional connection to people usually only comes with two settings: on or off. Try to add a few more settings or at least make sure everyone knows how you function so they don't conclude that you don't care.

Gemini rising combines your Virgo mind to make you adept at writing spells and rituals that make good use of correspondences and symbols. This rising helps your energy and aura stretch farther and adapt to whatever it touches. You would do well to develop your receptive psychic skills as well as practices such as mediumship and channeling.

You can pick up too much information and it can be overwhelming. Learn to close and control your awareness of other people's thoughts and feelings. You may have a gift for interpreting dreams and the words that come from oracles and seers. This combination often has a knack for knowing how best to use music, chanting, and drumming in magick.

Cancer Rising

You are more easily hurt than most Virgos, though you still manage to shine and seem untroubled. You show caring through material gestures, such as food, gifts, the gift of your time, and the opening of your heart. You are an excellent listener and rarely give advice, but when you do, it is gentle and precise. Virgo and Cancer are both interested in helping people, but they both also have a limited amount of time before they are done with being around people. You want to go with your gut most of the time, but that is not a good idea. Choose to use your intellect so you are not ruled by your emotions. An even mix of head and heart will steer you right.

You have a love of history, anthropology, folklore, genealogy, museums, and such. This can bring you great joy and activities that you treasure your whole life. These interests may shape your career choices. You need to blow your own horn more often. You get things done so smoothly that your efforts aren't always noticed. In matters of love, you make sure you find someone who is as sentimental as you are. The health of your gut and digestion is strongly affected by your emotional state; use it as an indicator to attend to your distress.

Cancer grants the power to use your emotions, or the emotional energy of others, to power your witchcraft. Though you can draw on a wide range of energies to fuel your magick, raising power through emotion is the simplest. You may also have a calling for dreamwork, past-life recall, or dowsing. Moon magick for practical workings for abundance or healing of the heart comes easily for you. Color magick, such as the choice of colors for candles, altar cloths, robes, banners, and color visualization, can also serve you well.

Leo Rising

The contrast between the two styles of Virgo and Leo means you stand out and are often the center of attention. With Leo rising, you tend to create the emotional and spiritual weather around you. When you are not doing well, things turn stormy. Center yourself and those around you will be calmer and happier. Seeing the impact you have on others may lead you to relying on people's reactions and feedback to monitor your state of being. Check in with your inner self instead and you'll thrive. Overall, you know how to manage your finances, but you will have the occasional bout of Leo-inspired spending. You may be drawn to work in finance, healthcare, or education. Public service is also a possible career path.

You are a loyal friend and tend to forgive offenses swiftly, though you never forget them. Be as kind to yourself as you are to others. In matters of love and friendship, you are a bit complicated to understand. Outwardly you look confident, but internally you have many worries and doubts. Be patient as those close to you get to see and understand your inner self. You prefer quality over quantity in most things in life.

Leo rising means that when you reach out to draw in power, fire will answer easily. Lean in to your Virgo mutability to shape fire and to focus it. Air and water answer your call through the power of your Sun and not your rising sign. Focus on the flexibility in your energy and imagination to access all the elements. Your aura and energy are brighter and steadier than most people's, so you attract the attention of spirits, deities, and so on. Whether or not showing up so clearly in the otherworlds is a gift or a challenge is up to you. Your Sun and rising give you a knack for healing work.

Virgo Rising

Virgo on top of more Virgo means you make a more serious impression on people. You are more precise in your word choices and actions. You are a keen observer of the world and notice the pertinent details.

When you are doing well, you are discerning, and when you are frustrated, you become hypercritical. When you are overwrought, your verbal criticisms can cut beyond the bone and all the way to the soul. You have a strong intellect and you can scan, cram, and sort information with speed and skill. It does make you a bit crazy when you must engage in group efforts when you are sure you'd be better off doing it all yourself.

You love your interests and projects as much as you do people. So, to have successful close relationships, you need people who are comfortable with the amount of space you need. Ideally, they also have many projects of their own. In your personal life and your work life, be watchful against focusing on the flaws and errors. You can get caught up in some really nonproductive cycles of thoughts and feelings. It is also important to know that sometimes you do have to bend or break the rules for better outcomes.

Virgo rising with a Virgo Sun makes it easier to work with goddesses and gods who are connected to the element of earth, plant life, agriculture, academic pursuits, or death work. You have a knack for creating connections between different kinds of magick and making them combine. Magickal research, divination, oracular work, and healing work are favored by this combination. Be careful when you entwine your energy with someone else's because you can pick up and retain their patterns and issues. Always cleanse your energy after doing solo or collective work.

♎

Libra Rising

You know how to sound, what to wear, and how to pull off all the little nonverbal cues of a culture, scene, or in-group. It does cost you energy to do this, but it is one of your superpowers. Your warmth can melt away most icy obstacles. Your weakness is that you are much more sensitive and shyer than you appear on the surface. It is not long until you need some alone time to recharge. Learning to take risks in small, measured steps to build courage will improve all parts of your life. You have many talents, but they have to be seen to be appreciated. Working it all in your head is not enough.

A messy or unlovely room can dampen your mood as fast as an impolite person. The reverse is also true in that beauty feeds you. Make sure you make the spaces you occupy as harmonious and lovely as you can manage. The more your day-to-day life matches your aesthetics, the more vitality you will have. Artistic activities that make use of your Virgo focus are enlivening for you. Your body responds quickly to your thoughts and feelings, so be kind to it.

Libra rising with a Virgo Sun wants to express its magick through the creation of things. You may carve and dress candles, create sumptuous altars, write beautiful invocations, or create amazing ritual wear. You also know how to bring together people who use different types of magick and arrange smooth collaborations. You are good at spell work for making peace, laying spirits to rest, attracting familiars, and self-love. Working with sound in magick and healing—whether it be voice, singing bowls, percussion, or an instrument—is also one of your gifts.

Scorpio Rising

This combination is intense, and your allure, air of mystery, and personal power are off the charts. You live in the moment, but you want to know all the details and backstory that lead to each moment. You want to be the best at whatever you do, whether that is work or play. If you feel blocked from reaching your goals, this combination can lead you to be seen as domineering or insensitive. Compromise does not come easily to you, but sarcasm does. When you give your heart to love, friendship, or a purpose, you do it fully and with great vigor. You can be a stalwart ally and defender, especially when the odds are not in your favor.

You are insightful and might do well as a lawyer, a planner, a therapist, a writer, and, of course, a witch. You are one of a kind and unforgettable. Virgo and Scorpio have different approaches to life, which creates an internal tension between cruel or kind, open or secretive, affectionate or aloof, and so on. Turn these tensions into shades of gray or, better yet, a full rainbow to access your power. Look to the rest of your chart, your life experience, and input from friends to find the middle ground when you lock up. You are an expert at asking questions and listening deeply.

Scorpio rising makes your energy capable of cutting through most energetic barriers. You can dissolve illusion or bring down wards or shields and see through to the truth. You may have an aptitude for breaking curses and lifting oppressive spiritual atmospheres. You could be a seer, but only if you learn emotional detachment. You have a knack for spells related to transformation, finding hidden or lost things, and revealing past lives. It is important that you do regular cleansing work for yourself. You are likely to end up doing messy work, and you do not have a nonstick aura.

Sagittarius Rising

This rising's enthusiasm and vision combined with your Sun's need to organize and work can make you great at whatever you choose to do. You also don't rest on your laurels for long. You take a victory lap and get back to work. The relentless Sagittarius energy combines well with conscientious Virgo. Both your Sun and rising are mutable, which gives you versatility and flexibility, but unless you keep centered, these can also lead to excess and spreading yourself too thin. Your personal life may deteriorate if you allow your projects to take over most of your time. You are responsible and conscientious in work matters; remember to be the same for friends and loved ones.

You love to travel and are equally interested in cultures, landscapes, and meeting new people. You have an unquenchable thirst to learn just about everything. Thankfully, you have an abundance of mental energy that is a passion of the mind. When you need to recharge fast, go outdoors; being outside lets you feel the interconnectedness of all living things. It is likely that you can turn off your emotions for the sake of clarity and efficiency. This is useful, but it may cause you to worry that you are coldhearted. This is not true unless you choose to always throttle back your feelings. If you did, your physical health would suffer as well.

Your magick is stronger when you are standing outside on the ground. Your rising sign's fire can become a pillar of flame in your hearth. Skill in the use and creation of ritual tools is favored by this combination because you can push your energy and intentions into objects with ease. You have a talent for rituals and spells that call forth creativity, wisdom, and freedom. If you do astral travel or soul journeying, be sure all of you is back and in its proper place.

Capricorn Rising

Ambition is strong in you, and you are methodical and relentless in your pursuit of success. This double earth combination encourages you to be practical, precise, and exacting. You are serious and stately, but you are not somber. You enjoy what the world has to offer more than most Virgos and are drawn to comfort and elegance. You do work harder and play less than most. Your challenge is to make sure that you keep a good balance in your life. It is easy for you to get so enthralled with your tasks that you neglect spending quality time with people who care about you. You can go long stretches without much human contact, but your humor and mood may turn dark and melancholy.

You are drawn to large-scale or long-term projects, and you are good at guiding and supporting people in these endeavors. You are good at keeping up to date with the changes in the world because you know that is needed to remain effective. You tend to be a stabilizing influence in the lives of those you interact with. In matters of love or close friendship, do not let worry over loss prevent you from sharing yourself with others. Also, those close to you do not judge you as severely as you do yourself.

Capricorn rising creates an aura and energy field that is slow to come up to speed but has amazing momentum once fully activated. Make it your habit to do some sort of energy work or meditative warm-up or breath work before engaging in witchcraft. Try working with crystals, stones, even geographic features like mountains as your magick blends well with them. Your rituals and spells benefit from having a structure and a plan of action. You are especially good at warding and spells to make long-term changes. You may have a commanding voice that the spirits hear.

♒

Aquarius Rising

There is a bit of a tug-of-war between a rising that loves thought and abstractions and a Virgo Sun that wants to keep things practical and grounded. Rather than being a problem, this dynamic tension gives you more energy to pursue your goals and tend to your duties. You have a sharp eye and can spot problems before they spin out of control and intervene to manage them. You approach most things in life with great verve and precision. You see the world very differently than most, and this gives you a quirky sense of humor. You also get joy from finding ways to circumvent the rules of the game of life.

This combination makes for original thinking and moments of genius. You seek social interaction for mental stimulation more so than for fun. Boredom will damage your health more than stress, so stay active. The Virgo side of this combination makes you more unpretentious, but your rigorous approach to things can make you hard to work with. However, when your role is providing support or service for someone, you are accommodating and conscientious. In matters of the heart, you are a little too cautious and not romantic in the usual way. When you do commit to friendship or love, you are devoted and steady in your connection and affection.

Aquarius rising helps you consciously change the shape and density of your aura. This makes you a generalist who can adapt to many styles and forms of magick. Witchcraft focused on increasing intuition, analysis of problems, and release from emotional restrictions is supported by this combination. Visualization can play an important role in your magick and meditations. If you aren't particularly good at visualization, focus the spoken word to tune in to your power. Aquarius rising is gifted at turning ideas into reality.

Pisces Rising

You come across as sympathetic, kind, and a touch otherworldly. Your Pisces-inspired psychic perceptions connect you with other people's feelings and thoughts. Your Virgo Sun gives you discernment to make this a gift rather than a challenge. Whether by logic or intuition, you find the simplest and most effective solutions to problems for other people or situations. If you are trying to solve your own problems, your idealism and fantasizing may get in the way. There are many who would gladly come to your aid. You are guided and often protected, but don't make your spirit helpers work too hard. You can excel in a wide range of fields, but the ones that make you feel alive involve providing people with an experience that opens their hearts, minds, or spirits.

You are affectionate and want romance with all the bells and whistles. When you are in love, you open completely and are quite vulnerable. Unfortunately, you tend to cling to your memories of past experiences, which can affect your current relationships.

Work on letting things go and take your time in opening up to your partners. Those you count as family, you will defend until your last breath. Music, and the arts in general, is one of the best medicines for your body, mind, and spirit.

Pisces rising connects your Virgo Sun with the other planes of reality. Your power as a witch flows when you do magick to open the gates to the otherworlds. You have a special gift for creating sacred space and blessing places. You can do astral travel, hedge riding, and soul travel in all their forms with some training and practice. You can help others find their psychic gifts. You may have a knack for the healing arts, especially in modes that rely on herbalism or energy work.

A DISH FIT FOR A VIRGO: GROUNDING SEED BREAD WITH MAPLE BUTTER

Dawn Aurora Hunt

* * *

This recipe for a wholesome bread made from scratch includes pumpkin seeds, sesame seeds, and a touch of honey.

For you, Virgo, nothing is more centering than a project where your hard work and focus result in a rich reward. This hearty multiseed bread not only holds the power and energy of kinship and prosperity, but it is a labor of love start to finish. While the dough is rising, meditate on the process. For bread to properly form, it must be let to rest. Breathe into the process and use it as exemplary ritual for your own cycles of hard work and rest and their outcomes. This recipe is best made using a Dutch oven but can be easily adapted to use an oven-safe deep baking dish with a lid. Enjoy the fruits of your labor by enjoying this toothsome bread warm from the oven with maple butter.

This bread is vegetarian by nature. It is not recommended to substitute gluten-free flour in this recipe.

Ingredients:

- 1½ cups warm water
- 2 tablespoons raw unfiltered honey
- 1 packet active dry yeast
- 1 teaspoon salt
- 2 cups bread flour
- 1 cup whole wheat or rye flour
- 2 tablespoons each toasted sunflower seeds, toasted pumpkin seeds, mixed black and white sesame seeds, flax seeds (plus any extra for dusting on top of the bread)
- 2 tablespoons cornmeal (optional)

For the Maple Butter

- 1 stick butter, softened
- 1 tablespoon real maple syrup
- Pinch cinnamon
- ½ teaspoon brown sugar

Directions:

Make the maple butter by combining butter, maple syrup, cinnamon, and brown sugar in a small bowl. Cover and chill until ready to serve.

In a small bowl, combine warm water and honey. Stir until honey is dissolved and sprinkle the top with yeast. Set aside about five minutes until yeast begins to foam. In a large bowl, combine flour and salt and all the seeds. Gently stirring with a large spatula or wooden spoon, slowly stir in the yeast mixture until a very sticky dough forms. Cover with plastic wrap and let stand at room temperature (72 degrees Fahrenheit) for at least two hours or until about tripled in size. Line a work surface with parchment paper and sprinkle the center with cornmeal or flour and set aside. Sprinkle the dough with flour and fold it in half two or three times. Flour your hands well and lift the dough onto your prepared parchment paper. If desired, sprinkle more seeds on top of the dough. Let sit at room temperature to rise again, another sixty minutes. While the dough is on its second rise, preheat the oven to 450 degrees Fahrenheit with the empty Dutch oven and Dutch oven lid inside so they preheat as well. Remove the empty Dutch oven and lid from the oven carefully, using oven mitts. Lift the bread and the parchment into the center of the hot Dutch oven. Cover with the lid and bake for about thirty minutes or until the bread has formed a crust on top. For a crunchier top crust, remove the lid of the Dutch oven and let the bread bake an additional five minutes. Remove from the oven and let cool about five to ten minutes before slicing. Serve warm with maple butter or alongside soup.

RECHARGING AND SELF-CARE

Thumper Forge

more than anything else, Virgos need our "me" time—moments when we can just be quietly alone, without distraction or anyone else's emergencies clamoring for our attention.

The trick is actually *getting* some time to ourselves, since we put so much emphasis on taking care of the people around us. For me, this means applying the very important life lessons I learned from *Baywatch*.

Hear me out on this.

For those who weren't around at the time, *Baywatch* was an action-adventure prime-time drama that aired from 1989 to 2001. At one point, it was the most watched show in network television history, with more than one billion viewers worldwide. The plot centered around Lieutenant Mitch Buchannon, played by David Hasselhoff, leading a team of highly trained, unspeakably hot lifeguards who spent most of their workdays running in slow motion and having wind-swept hair.

I tuned in every week. Religiously.

In the third season finale, Australian lifeguard Wiley Brown transferred to Mitch's station on an exchange program and set about winning everyone over with his charm and daredevil attitude, all while attempting to creatively murder Mitch. As it turned out, many years prior, Mitch had rescued Wiley's wife Sheila during a windsurfing accident, but as he was pulling her to shore, he bumped into a piling and knocked himself out, thus allowing Sheila to drown.

There were a couple of big takeaways from this episode, the first being that I would never, ever be heterosexual. But, more importantly, it was revealed that a lifeguard should always put a given victim between themself and any obstacle they encounter in the ocean. If the victim gets banged up, they can still recover. But if the lifeguard gets injured, the chances of survival drop dramatically for both of them.

Even though I watched this episode as a teenager—and even though the message was analogous to putting on your own oxygen mask before helping anyone else with theirs—the inherent lesson didn't really hit me until I was in my early forties. Prior to then, I'd kind of made it my mission in life to Save Everyone, while putting little to no effort into my own well-being—lots of lugging around other people's emotional baggage so that I wouldn't have to unpack my own.

I quit drinking back in 2012, which helped tremendously, but in early sobriety, I was pretty bad about taking on responsibilities at the expense of self-care. So I was participating in multiple organizations and running two covens and acting as pro bono therapist for numerous friends, and since so many people were depending on me, I was reluctant to reach out when I needed to lean on somebody.

I have since developed some tips and tricks to navigate this. But at the time, without those tools at hand, I had to learn how to channel Big Lifeguard Energy and set some boundaries. If I was at a social function, say, and an anxiety attack was about to hit, I would simply leave. I would do my best to tell someone what was going on, just so that no one would worry, but if they were like, "Oh, you'll be fine, stay five more minutes," I would be like, "Nope, see ya," and bail. And if they got butthurt about it, that was their problem—I could deal with it when I was in a better mindset.

And, y'all, I know everyone reading this is like, "What the hell does *Baywatch* have to do with being a Virgo witch?!" But I promise I have a point. In fact, want to know who the first Virgo was to apply *Baywatch* thinking to her own circumstances, albeit via retroactive continuity? The Goddess

Astraea, who is literally the *original* Virgo. So, yeah, there's totally precedence here.

Astraea is a goddess of the stars and of justice, closely associated with other judicial deities like Dike and Themis. As one of the oldest of the immortals, Astraea was around during the Golden Age, when the gods lived among humans.

I started to say, "Lived in harmony with humans," but that wasn't really the case. Humanity's base nature started to kind of eat away at Astraea's peace of mind, and as the human race got more aggressive and debaucherous, Astraea finally snapped and was like, "I am *no longer* having this," and promptly turned herself into a constellation to get away from everyone.

Let's take a moment to really consider the *chutzpah* of her actions. In other religions, when the gods get disgusted with humankind, they send floods or plagues or whatever to deal with the problem. On the other hand, when Astraea hit a breaking point, she was just like, "Nope," and bailed. Like, she left the entire population of ancient Greece on read.

And now she's up in the night sky, watching over us … much like a lifeguard. But she also took care of herself before taking care of anyone else. And if *she* can do it, as the progenitor of the stars that make up our Sun sign, so can we.

A Virgo Lifeguard Meditation

Just before you're ready to go to sleep, stretch out on your bed with a pillow next to you and picture yourself in the ocean with the night sky full of stars above you. You're floating toward the shore, along with another person (the pillow) who is dependent on you for survival.

Once you can feel the buoyancy of the water and the weight of the person next to you, visualize a large object looming in front of you: a pylon or a dock jutting out into the water. Feel yourself moving steadily toward it—it's big enough so that you're not going to be able to avoid or swim around it.

As you draw closer, grasp your pillow and pull it in front of your chest. The person you're guiding to shore is now between you and the object. Feel the cushioned impact as they bump into the object with a soft *oof*—the contact is jarring, but not life-threatening. The two of you roll around the object and continue swimming toward land, and you very quickly feel sand beneath your feet. Help the other person onto the shore, then lie down on the beach, look up at the sky, and notice how the stars seem a bit brighter, as if Astraea is nodding in approval. Feel the ground beneath you shift back into your bed as you drift off to sleep.

Repeat this meditation every night until pulling the pillow between you and the object you're visualizing is instinctive and second nature. And then, the next time you need to remove yourself from a situation, summon up that feeling, and know that you're doing what's best for everyone involved, superficial bruises to any egos notwithstanding.

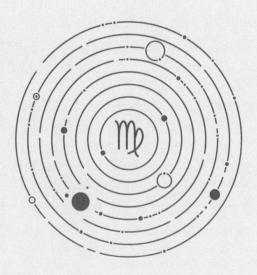

Navigating Overindulgence

Now, here's the thing, my Virgin siblings: there is not a doubt in my mind that some of you read the paragraphs above and immediately hopped online to locate a handcrafted, free trade, weighted body pillow with a pentagram on it to incorporate into your meditation. And what will happen next is that you'll find several hundred pillows that are *almost* but *not quite* right, but you'll eventually discover the Holy Grail of Body Pillows, and you'll be desperate to own it, but it'll be *just* a bit out of your price range, so you'll agonize over that for a week or six months or so, until you'll finally snap and make the purchase, which will be followed instantaneously by crippling regret over the money you've just spent on yourself.

So hey, listen. A pillow you already have will work perfectly. I promise. And also, if it's going to make us feel guilty, overindulgence won't cut it as self-care.

This is not to say that we can't have nice things, or that we don't deserve nice things—we absolutely do. And because we're Virgos, our nice things are very important to us. But if the process of obtaining the things is going to send us into a spiral of overthinking, we would do well to pull a *Baywatch* and paddle away.

Of course, we're occasionally going to come across an item that's hard to resist. To prevent an onslaught of shopping-related neuroses, we can control the variables by limiting ourselves to four simple questions:

+ Is it reasonably priced?
+ Do I have a place for it?
+ Do I have a use for it?
+ Am I trying to change how I feel?

That last question is crucial. As Virgos, we are solution-based, but we tend to be a lot more commonsensical when solving other people's problems than when dealing with our own. Spending money to change our emotional state may seem like a quick fix, but it's ultimately just a bandage that will eventually peel off; whatever issues we're trying to ignore will still be festering underneath it. So let's always make sure we're in a good place mentally and emotionally before adding anything to our carts, just so that we're not tossing buyer's remorse into the already jumbled psychic salad.

Just like I wouldn't walk into a ritual if I wasn't feeling 100 percent good to go, I'm not going to stroll into a retail establishment, debit card set to vaporize, if my Virgo brain is fixated on immediate gratification over legitimate self-care. And I'm never going to push myself too hard whenever I know I don't have the resources to do much more than manage my basic needs. But I also know that if I take time for myself, to rest and recover, I inevitably end up splashing about in the brine before I know it. At which point I'm not going to feel badly about treating myself a little.

And if you're not feeling in top form, or you're struggling with outside demands on your time, I promise it's okay to take a break and pay attention to yourself for a while. I promise you that there are plenty of life preservers to go around until you've officially returned to duty. Astraea totally has your back on this one.

The Gift of Nature's Balance
Self-Care for Virgos

Stephanie Rose Bird

I've been aware of being a Virgo for about as long as I've been involved with the Craft—decades. My relationship with that is both uneasy and positive depending on my outlook and situation. I notice some of the more challenging attributes of the sign and their ability to derail my day. I'm talking about the perfectionism and single-mindedness for which we are known. Virgos can be type A personality, overly critical, and the dreaded overthinkers. The cool thing is we are also earthy, deep-rooted, and grounded people with a high level of creativity expressed through the arts. Moreover, our sign embodies the Great Goddess. Now, just how auspicious is that?

With Earth Mama's gifts of flowers, we can do many things: heal, cure, redirect attention, bring cheer, restore balance, and strengthen the spirit. My chosen method of self-care flower magick for you, Virgo, is Bach's Flower Remedies. These magickal elixirs are thinly veiled potions. They contain a wide array of magickal powers. Homeopathy addresses dis-ease of the mind, body, and spirit, using pulverized and dispersed curatives—such as herbs (in our case, flowers), minerals, and parts of animals—extracted into a liquid. They are taken by the drop.

You will need:

- **White Chestnut Bach Flower Remedy.** White chestnut addresses the type A personality by bringing tranquility to the mind. With a calm mind, you create a bridge that travels from Virgo overthinking to our grounded and rooted personality. Once you cross the bridge from one way of thinking to another, you gain freedom to be easier on yourself and others.

- **Clematis Bach Flower Remedy.** Clematis knows you are enveloped in perfectionism and constant critiques. This busyness makes it easy to lose concentration because one thought leads to another. The magick of clematis is its ability to redirect your attention and instill focus.

- **Scleranthus Bach Flower Remedy.** With calm and concentration already invoked, you are empowered. It's nice to be open to choices, but there comes the time for decisiveness, and that is the gift of scleranthus.

Find a peaceful, safe, and secluded location. This could be outdoors, in the forest, on a beach, in a meadow, or atop a hill. If these locations don't work for you, simulate them. Find earth sounds to listen to from your preferred environment.

Sites such as YouTube offer these sounds. I like listening to birdsongs, crickets, fires, and ocean waves.

Comfortable, as you happily soak in your environment, take two drops of each Flower Remedy. I like the sublingual technique of dropping them under my tongue. Repeat this activity thrice, spread out through the day. Alternately, drop six drops of each Flower Remedy in a water bottle of spring water and sip while in your meditative environment, all day until finished.

To take this spell work deeper, add the following incantations.

> First Sips (White Chestnut)
> *I am open. My mind is settled down.*
> *I relinquish tension and stress.*
>
> Second Sips (Clematis)
> *I welcome decidedness.*
> *I now know what I want to do.*
>
> Third Sips (Scleranthus)
> *I see a clear path. I embody my direction.*
> *Ashe-ashe, ashe-ashe!*
> *Blessed be!*

Recite thrice, along with taking the elixirs.

DON'T BLAME IT ON YOUR SUN SIGN

Thumper Forge

A coworker and I recently discovered that our birthdays fall about a week apart, and since I was working on this book, I decided to throw a pop quiz at him.

"So, as a Virgo," I asked, "If I were to say to you, 'No, thanks, I don't need any help,' what would be the next words out of my mouth?"

And my coworker grinned, leaned back, and bellowed, "WHY ISN'T ANYONE HELPING ME?!"

This, to me, is both the most amusing and the most disastrous thing about being a Virgo. When someone blames an aspect of their personality on their Sun sign, our skepticism rivals that of Capricorns. But when there's something about *ourselves* that we're not entirely willing to change, we're immediately like, "Oh, there's nothing I can do about that. It's because I'm a Virgo."

It's when someone offers us help that we suddenly latch on to our Sun sign in a death grip and claim that the powers of astrology are immutable.

So you know what? Let's just really embrace our Virgoness and look at why we don't like accepting help:

- There's no such thing as a free lunch; offers of help come with strings attached.
- Someone might mean well when they offer to help, but they're just going to do everything incorrectly, which means we're going to have to redo it all.
- Accepting help means accepting that we can't do everything by ourselves, which means that we have *failed at life*.

The reality is that none of the above is actually true, although that third one certainly feels true a lot of the time. It's tough to admit that we can't do it all by ourselves, and for a Virgo, accepting help can sometimes trigger feelings of inadequacy instead of gratitude.

But what's even tougher than accepting help for us Virgins is asking for help in the first place.

I'll tell you, the times in my life when I've gotten in the most trouble were incidents where things would've worked out just fine if I'd asked for help when I realized I was going to need it, instead of waiting until a given catastrophe hit. And when friends and family would ask why I didn't reach out to anyone, even though I knew there were problems I couldn't overcome on my own, I would be like, "I refuse to be a bother," or, "I should've been able to handle it," or, *You know I don't like asking for help.*

In other words, "Because I'm a Virgo."

Part of the problem is that, as Virgos, we expect everyone around us to react as if they were Virgos, too. For instance, if I see a coworker struggling with something, I just go help them. If I ask them anything before I jump in, it's usually something like, "What can I do?" or, "Where would you like me to start?" And I tend to assume that other people will do the same for me. Except I generally don't broadcast when I'm struggling, so the people around me are usually like, "Well, he's obviously got this situation under control," even when I'm internally flailing and dangerously close to losing my shit.

There's a scene in the movie *Boys on the Side* in which the character Robin says, "Between me and everybody else there's all this space all the time, and it gets bigger and bigger and, I'm on one side, and I'm screaming, and they're waving."[2]

---

2. Herbert Ross, *Boys on the Side* (Burbank, CA: Warner Brothers, 1995), 115 min.

I feel like a lot of Virgos will sympathize with this, especially when we're having crises. We're giving off what we think are *extremely clear and understandable* indications that we desperately need some kind of backup, but what everyone sees is us just being capable and on top of things, like the tried-and-true Virgos they know us to be.

So here's what we're going to do about it: we're going to step away from our Sun sign, get rid of that space between us and everyone else, and magic ourselves into witches who can ask for some help every now and again.

All we really need for this bit of ritual is a small bell—a handheld one, a pair of tingshas, or even one of those little circular call bells you find on reception desks. On a Sunday evening, place the bell on your altar and get comfy in front of it. Center yourself with a few slow, deep breaths, and picture that space between you and others as a wall: thick and mortared, but old and brittle. Once you've got the wall depicted in your mind's eye, pick up your bell and ring it three times, paying direct attention to the vibrations that emanate from it.

As the vibrations reach you and move through you, direct them at the wall you've been picturing. Every time sound hits it, a chink opens up, and light shines through. Ring the bell three more times, see the holes in the wall get wider, and feel more light blaze through.

Keep up this visualization for as long as you can, ringing your bell three times every few minutes until most, if not all, of the wall you've imagined has been demolished. Once complete, place the bell back on your altar, noting the tingle of the vibrations still in the air and the warmth of the light on your skin.

Try this mini ritual every night for a week, until the sensations of tingle and warmth are familiar enough that you can recall them at will. And I want you to recall them, not when you're at your wit's end and about to have a meltdown, but at the specific moment it hits you that you're going to need help with something.

Let's say you've got a work project due in a month. A week into the project, you realize that you're going to need support in order to make the deadline. Instead of waiting for three weeks and six days to bring that up, summon your projective vibration and your receptive glow, and then—and this is the important part—*go ask for help right then and there.*

The vibration will allow you to vocalize your need for help; the glow will draw that help to you. Once both have been accomplished, and when you have a moment to yourself, take a few seconds to enjoy the pride and relief that comes with the realization that you both asked for and accepted assistance. And nobody died because you did so.

Our fear of asking for help, of course, is rooted firmly in the control freak core of our Virgo personalities. We want to stay in control; allowing someone to help us introduces variables into the equation. We kind of hate that, and it's another instance where we'll fall back on "I'm a Virgo, I can't help it" rather than admit that *[deep breath]* we can't actually control everything everywhere all at once.

I know. It sucks to hear that. But here's the fun paradox of being Virgos: we have total control over whether or not we think we can control everything. The trick is learning to let go—that is, to pry our fingers off the *need* to control everything.

To start working on this, we can borrow a tool from 12-Step Recovery, the Third Step of which is, "Made the decision to turn our will and our lives over to the care of [the] God[s] as we understood Him [or Her, or Them, or the Universe, or however you perceive forces greater than yourself]." This step is not about giving up all control—rather, it's about acknowledging the difference between the things we do and do not have power over, and trusting the gods (or the universe, or our individual perceptions of whatever our higher powers are) to take care of the stuff that we, as humans, don't have the ability to oversee.

Something else we can use as we start the process of relaxing our grip is the concept of the Next Right Thing. Focusing on the Next Right Thing, especially in situations where we're feeling helpless or overwhelmed, not only gives us direction, but places emphasis on the things we do actually have the power to change, versus the things over which we realistically have no control.

A good friend of mine (and my original sponsor in 12-Step Recovery) used to explain the Next Right Thing in terms of zucchini bread. Let's say I've had an argument with my roommate, and the following morning, in a fit of rage, I take a loaf of his favorite zucchini bread and shove it down the garbage disposal. After doing so, I realize that I've over-reacted. I need to replace the bread, and I'm worried about getting that taken care of before he finds out what I've done, but I also need to clean myself up and go to work.

The Next Right Thing is to clean myself up and go to work. Once my workday is done, the Next Right Thing is to go to the store and buy more zucchini bread. I can figure out the Next Right Thing after that once I'm home, bread in hand.

Ultimately, we can't change the fact that we're Virgos. But as Virgo witches, we have abilities at our disposal to help us work around and redirect our more stereotypical traits. We're naturally suspicious, but we can turn that inward to look at the undercurrents of our quirks, versus second-guessing the motivations of anyone who wants to help us out. We're control freaks, but we can narrow that down to differentiate between what we can and can't control—and then we manage the things we can, and we get surprisingly nonchalant about the things we can't.

Above all else, don't forget that Virgo is a mutable sign. As Virgos, we can adapt and change to suit any situation in which we might find ourselves. But as Virgo witches, we can adapt and change internally as well, and become all the better for it. Sometimes that's going to look like sitting on the floor while clutching bits of metal and rock, and sometimes that's going to look like zucchini bread replaced with contrition. But regardless of the superficial appearance, what it is at its core is Virgos evolving into the Virgos we're supposed to be.

Or, if you prefer, Virgos evolving into the Virgos No One Saw Coming. And I hope that phrase brings you as much unmitigated satisfaction as it does me. So let's Next Right Thing our way toward that goal.

POSTCARD FROM A VIRGO WITCH

Gina Martini

There are so many wonderful (and not-so-wonderful) Virgo traits that present themselves throughout so much of my life in my relationships, magic, spirituality, or day job. The wonderful traits like being practical, industrious, humble, creative, patient, kind, and reliable are where I outwardly shine. Those not-so-wonderful traits (critical, stubborn, picky, uptight, and overthinking) when I notice them and work through them are where I inwardly shine.

The best way I feel I can show all my Virgo goodness (and not so goodness) is describing when I ran a festival in Connecticut called Harvest Gathering. It's a pretty big event: two hundred people for a weekend of camping, rituals, workshops, catered food, fire circle, and general fun.

As a Virgo, the trait that seems to be in my favor is organizing events; I love every part of it and throw myself into the work from the ground up. Yes, there are logistics of spreadsheets, meetings, emails, airline tickets, clerical work, and all the tasty business details. This Virgo loves the details; it's the little details that make it feel like the event is touched by divinity and spark inspiration for the guests. There is also the creative side, coming up with a theme of the event. Planning the presentations and speakers is where I admit to being picky because I felt it was important to get the right people to continue the magical intention. I have high standards with my staff too; I made sure we had the very best people and that they felt what we were doing was important.

We had planning sessions to think up ways to make the experience for each guest feel magical and transforming. One of the ideas I came up with is having a key phrase or thing that could be linked to magic and used year after year. That later took on a life of its own from the amazing staff I had the honor to work with as a simple phrase of greeting everyone with "welcome home." It was just the right detail that made this Virgo over the Moon.

Once all the preparation was done, I was getting in there at the event and being present, really present. Talking to everyone and making sure they felt welcomed, that they were cared for, special, and that this is and was "home." That was a lot of staying up late and getting up before the Sun for the whole event. I never left the event; I felt I had to be there, and that was important. A labor of love and, honestly, some of the best experiences I've had to see other people's joy, transformation, and bliss.

I'm sure you are thinking, <u>Wow, everything was roses and rainbows</u>. A lot of it was, and a lot of it wasn't. This is where Virgo patience and kindness is a blessing. You can shift your perspective when the not-so-great moments are the opportunities to grow as a person, as a team, and as a community.

SPIRIT OF VIRGO GUIDANCE RITUAL

Ivo Dominguez, Jr.

The signs are more than useful constructs in astrology or categories for describing temperaments; they are also powerful and complicated spiritual entities. So, what is meant when we say that a sign is a spirit? I often describe the signs of the zodiac as the twelve forms of human wisdom and folly. The signs are twelve styles of human consciousness, which also means that the signs are well-developed group minds and egregores. Think on the myriad of people over thousands of years who have poured energy into the constructs of the signs through intentional visualization and study. Moreover, the lived experience of each person as one of the signs is deposited into the group minds and egregores of their sign. Every Virgo who has ever lived or is living contributes to the spirit of Virgo.

The signs have a composite nature that allows them to exist in many forms on multiple planes of reality at once. In addition to the human contribution to their exis-tence, the spirits of the signs are made from inputs from all living beings in our world whether they are made of dense matter or spiritual substances. These vast and ancient thoughtforms that became group minds and then egregores are also vessels that can be used by divine beings to communicate with humans. The spirits of the signs can manifest themselves as small as a sprite or larger than the Earth. The shape and the magnitude of the spirit of Virgo that emerges before you will depend on who you are and how and why you call upon them.

Purpose and Use

This ritual will make it possible to commune with the spirit of Virgo. The form that the spirit will take will be different each time you perform the ritual. What appears will be determined by what you are looking for and your state of mind and soul. The process for preparing yourself for the ritual will do you good as well. Aligning yourself with the source and core of your energy is a useful practice in and of itself. Exploring your circumstances, motivations, and intentions is a valuable experience whether or not you are performing this ritual.

If you have a practical problem that you are trying to solve or an obstacle that must be overcome, the spirit of Virgo may have useful advice. If you are trying to better understand who you are and what you are striving to accomplish, then the spirit of Virgo can be your mentor. Should you have a need to recharge yourself or flush out stale energy, you can use this ritual to reconnect with a strong, clear current of power that is compatible with your core. This energy can be used for magickal empowerment, physical vitality, or healing or redirected for spell work. If you are charging objects or magickal implements with Virgo energy, this ritual can be used for this purpose as well.

Timing for the Ritual

The prevailing astrological conditions have an impact on how you experience a ritual, the type and amount of power available, and the outcomes of the work. If you decide you want to go deeper in your studies of astrology, you'll find many techniques to pick the best day and time for your ritual.

Thankfully, the ritual to meet the spirit of your sign does not require exact timing or perfect astrological conditions. This ritual depends on your inner connection to your Sun sign, so it is not as reliant on the external celestial conditions as some other rituals. Each of us has worlds within ourselves, which include inner landscapes and inner skies. Your birth chart, and the sky that it depicts, shines brightest within you. Although not required, you can improve the effectiveness of this ritual if you use any of the following simple guidelines for favorable times:

+ When the Moon or the Sun is in Virgo.
+ When Mercury is in Virgo.
+ On Wednesday, the day of Mercury, and even better at dawn, which is its planetary hour.
+ The day before the equinox before the Sun moves to Libra.

Materials and Setup

The following is a description of the physical objects that will make it easier to perform this ritual. Don't worry if you don't have all of them; in a pinch, you need no props. However, the physical objects will help anchor the energy and your mental focus.

You will need:

- A printout of your birth chart
- A table to serve as an altar
- A chair if you want to sit during the ritual
- A small dish or tray filled with small twigs or leaves to represent the element of earth
- An assortment of items for the altar that correspond to Virgo or Mercury (for example, a moss agate, a sprig of cypress or dill, Mercury dime, and a chrysanthemum or jonquil)
- A pad and a pen or chalk and a small blackboard, or something else you can use to draw a glyph

Before beginning the ritual, you may wish to copy the ritual invocations onto paper or bookmark this chapter and bring the book into the ritual. I find that the process of writing out the invocation, whether handwritten or typed, helps forge a better connection with the words and their meaning.

If possible, put the altar table in the center of your space, or as close to due east as you can manage. Place the dish with the twigs on the altar and hold your hand over it. Send warming energy from your hand to the twigs. Put your birth chart on the altar to one side of the twigs and arrange the items you have selected to anchor the Virgo and Mercury energy around it. To the other side of the dish, place the writing implements. Make sure you turn off your phone, close the door, close the curtains, or do whatever else is needed to prevent distractions.

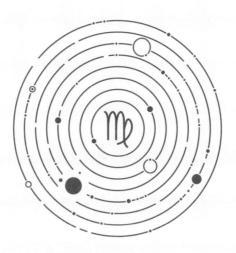

Ritual to Meet the Spirit of Your Sign

You may stand or be seated—whichever is most comfortable for you. Begin by focusing on your breathing. When you pay attention to the process of breathing, you become more aware of your body, the flow of your life energy, and the balance between conscious and unconscious actions. After you have done so for about a minute, it is time to shift into fourfold breathing. This consists of four phases: inhaling, lungs full, exhaling, and lungs empty. You count to keep time so that each of the four phases is of equal duration. Try a count of four or five in your first efforts. Depending on your lungs and how fast you count, you will need to adjust the number higher or lower. When you hold your breath, hold it with your belly muscles, not your throat. When you hold your breath in fourfold breathing, your throat should feel relaxed. Be gentle and careful with yourself if you have asthma or high blood pressure, are late in pregnancy, or have any other condition that may impact your breathing and blood pressure. In general, if there are difficulties, they arise during the lungs full or empty phases because of holding the breath by clenching the throat or compressing the lungs. The empty and full lungs should be held by the position of the diaphragm, and the air passages left open. After one to three minutes of fourfold breathing, you can return to your normal breathing pattern.

Now close your eyes and move your center of consciousness down into the middle of your chest. Proceed with grounding and centering, dropping and opening, shifting into the alpha state, or whatever practice you use to reach the state of mind that supports ritual work. Then gaze deeply inside yourself and find yourself sitting on the ground in a garden. Look at the beauty of the plants, their leaves and flowers. Take a breath and smell fresh air and sweet fragrances. Dig your fingers gently into the rich earth and awaken all the places and spaces within you that are of Virgo. When you feel ready, open your eyes.

Zodiac Casting

If you are seated, stand if you are able and face the east. Slowly read this invocation aloud, putting some energy into your words. As you read, slowly turn counterclockwise so that you come full circle when you reach the last line. Another option is to hold your hand over your head and trace the counterclockwise circle of the zodiac with your finger.

I call forth the twelve to join me in this rite.
I call forth Aries and the power of courage.
I call forth Taurus and the power of stability.
I call forth Gemini and the power of versatility.
I call forth Cancer and the power of protection.
I call forth Leo and the power of the will.
I call forth Virgo and the power of discernment.
I call forth Libra and the power of harmony.
I call forth Scorpio and the power of renewal.
I call forth Sagittarius and the power of vision.
I call forth Capricorn and the power of responsibility.
I call forth Aquarius and the power of innovation.
I call forth Pisces and the power of compassion.
The power of the twelve is here.
Blessed be!

Take a few deep breaths and gaze at the dish of twigs. Become aware of the changes in the atmosphere around you and the presence of the twelve signs.

Altar Work

Pick up the printout of your birth chart and look at your chart. Touch each of the twelve houses with your finger and push energy into them. You are energizing and awakening your birth chart to act as a focal point of power on the altar. Put your chart back on the altar when it feels ready to you. Then take the pad and pen and write the glyph for Virgo again and again. The glyphs can be different sizes, they can overlap; you can make any pattern with them you like so long as you pour energy into the ink as you write. Scribing the glyph is an action that helps draw the interest of the spirit of Virgo. Periodically look at the twigs as you continue scribing the glyph. When you feel sensations in your body such as electric tingles, warmth, shivers, or something that you associate with the approach of a spirit, it is time to move on to the next step. If these are new experiences for you, just follow your instincts. Put away the pen and paper and pick up the sheet with the invocation of Virgo.

Invoking Virgo

Before beginning to read this invocation, get in touch with your feelings. Think on what you hope to accomplish in this ritual and why it matters to you. Then speak these lines slowly and with conviction.

> *Virgo, hear me, for I am born of the green world's mutable earth.*
> *Virgo, see me, for the Virgo Sun shines upon me.*
> *Virgo, know me as a member of your family and your company.*
> *Virgo, know me as your student and your protégé.*
> *Virgo, know me as a conduit for your power.*
> *Virgo, know me as a wielder of your magick.*
> *I am of you, and you are of me.*
> *I am of you, and you are of me.*
> *I am of you, and you are of me.*
> *Virgo is here, within and without.*
> *Blessed be!*

Your Requests

Now look inward for several deep breaths, and, silently or aloud, welcome the spirit of Virgo. Pick up and hold one of the twigs. Close your eyes and ask for any guidance that would be beneficial for you and listen. It may take some time before anything comes through, so be patient. I find it valuable to receive guidance before making a request so that I can refine or modify intentions and outcomes. Consider the meaning of whatever impressions or guidance you received and reaffirm your intentions and desired outcomes for this ritual.

It is more effective to use multiple modes of communication to make your request. Speak silently or aloud the words that describe your need and how it could be solved. Visualize the same message but without the words and project the images on your mind's screen. Then put all your attention on your feelings and your bodily sensations that have been stirred up by contemplating your appeal to the spirit of Virgo. Once again, wait and use all your physical and psychic senses to perceive what is given. At this point in the ritual, if there are objects to be charged, touch them or focus your gaze on them.

Offer Gratitude

You may be certain or uncertain about the success of the ritual or the time frame for the outcomes to become clear. Regardless of that, it is a good practice to offer thanks and gratitude to the spirit of Virgo for being present. Also, thank yourself for doing your part of the work. The state of heart and mind that comes with thanks and gratitude makes it easier for the work to become manifest. Thanks and gratitude also act as a buffer against the unintended consequences that can be put into motion by rituals.

Release the Ritual

If you are seated, stand if you are able and face the east. Slowly turn clockwise until you come full circle while repeating the following or something similar.

Return, return oh turning wheel to your starry home.
Farewell, farewell oh Virgo bright until we speak again.

Another option while saying these words is to hold your hand over your head and trace a clockwise circle of the zodiac with your finger. When you are done, snuff out the candle on the altar and say,

It is done. It is done. It is done.

Afterward

I encourage you to write down your thoughts and observations of what you experienced in the ritual. Do this while it is still fresh in mind before the details begin to blur. The information will become more useful over time as you work more with the spirit of Virgo. It will also let you evaluate the outcomes of your workings and improve your process in future workings. This note-taking or journaling will also help you dial in any changes or refinements to this ritual for future use. Contingent upon the guidance you received or the outcomes you desire, you may want to add reminders to your calendar.

More Options

These are some modifications to this ritual that you may wish to try:

* Put together or purchase Virgo incense to burn during the ritual. A Virgo oil to anoint the twigs and leaves or yourself is another possibility. I'm providing one of my oil recipes as a possibility.

+ Set up a richer and deeper altar. In addition to adding more objects that resonate to the energy of Virgo or Mercury, consecrate each object before the ritual. You may also want to place an altar cloth on the table that suggests Virgo, Mercury, or the element of earth.

+ Creating a sigil to concentrate the essence of what you are working toward would be a good addition to the altar.

+ Consider adding chanting, free-form toning, or movement to raise energy for the altar work and/or for invoking Virgo.

+ If you feel inspired, you can write your own invocations for calling the zodiac and/or invoking Virgo. This is a great way to deepen your understanding of the signs and to personalize your ritual.

Rituals have greater personal meaning and effectiveness when you personalize them and make them your own.

VIRGO ANOINTING OIL RECIPE

✳ ✳ ✳

Ivo Dominguez, Jr.

This oil is used for charging and consecrating candles, crystals, and other objects you use in your practice. This oil makes it easier for an object to be imbued with Virgo energy. It also primes and tunes the objects so that your will and power as a Virgo witch flow more easily into them. Do not apply the oil to your skin unless you have done an allergy test first.

Ingredients:

+ Carrier oil—1 ounce
+ Patchouli—5 drops
+ Petitgrain—6 drops
+ Cypress—6 drops
+ Sandalwood—2 drops
+ Myrrh—4 drops

Pour one ounce of a carrier oil into a small bottle or vial. The preferred carrier oils are almond oil or fractionated coconut oil. Other carrier oils can be used. If you use olive oil, the blend will have a shorter shelf life. Ideally use essential oils, but fragrance oils can be used as substitutes. Add the drops of the essential oils into the carrier. Once they are all added, cap the bottle tightly and shake the bottle several times. Hold the bottle in your hands, take a breath, and pour energy into the oil. Visualize green energy or repeat the word *Virgo* or raise energy in your preferred manner. Continue doing so until the oil feels warm, seems to glow, or you sense it is charged.

Label the bottle and store the oil in a cool, dark place. Consider keeping a little bit of each previous batch of oil to add to the new batch. This helps build the strength and continuity of the energy and intentions you have placed in the oil. Over time, that link makes your oils more powerful.

BETTER EVERY DAY: THE WAY FORWARD

Thumper Forge

I kind of have to laugh at myself when I look back over my occult career, because the vast majority of it involves me saying things like, "Oh, you want to change jobs? I've got a ritual for that." "Oh, you're dealing with mild but constant joint pain? Let's do some magic about it." "Oh, you've got a vengeful ex-boyfriend? Bring me a recent picture and some black ribbon." And then someone will say, "You know, Thumper, you seem a bit strapped for cash. Why don't you come over this weekend, and we'll do a money spell?" And I'll be like, "Oh, no, thanks. I'm going to take out a high-interest, predatory payday loan instead."

It's probably just because we're so invested in putting others before ourselves, but Virgo witches are the *worst* about not using witchcraft to improve our own circumstances. Like, the last time someone asked me to cast a job spell for them, I showed up at their place with candles and home-brewed incense and freshly made oils and witchcrafted the damn house down, and they were gainfully reemployed within a week. However, the last time I was let go from a job, I ended up unemployed for three months. And while I did eventually get hired by a great company where I love working, it took me two and a half months to get off my ass and cast the spell that landed me the job.

In this book, we've explored divination, binding, setting firm boundaries, and opening up to outside assistance. So now it's time to move forward—and in order to do that, we're going to start casting spells for ourselves.

I know. It feels counterintuitive. But sometimes, people have no choice but to put themselves first. Even Virgos.

A big part of this is going to be building up our own self-confidence around self-serving spell work. I never really fret about spells when I cast them for other people—like, when I did the work to get my friend a new job, there was not a doubt in my mind that said job would present itself quickly (and it did). But when it comes to spells for my own benefit … yeah, that's when the self-doubt kicks in.

Did I use the most appropriate herbs? Did I light enough candles? Did I employ the right colors and correspondences?

Did I draw that sigil correctly? Basically, casting a spell for someone else involves me nodding confidently and saying, "Yes, it'll work," whereas casting a spell for myself is like, "Yes, it'll work, *as long as I did everything perfectly*."

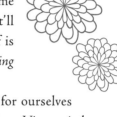

It's those higher standards we have for ourselves getting in the way again, holding us back as Virgo witches when we're supposed to be moving forward. So let's clear that obstacle once and for all with some foolproof woo.

A Spell to Attract Money

And no, not, like, a ton of money—we're not trying to win the lottery or anything. This is just an easy spell to bring in a little extra cash—enough to let our deep minds know that the spells we cast for ourselves can have just as much real-world impact as the spells we cast for friends and family.

You will need:

+ A Mercury dime. (The image on the head of a Mercury dime is actually Young Liberty, but she's depicted wearing a winged cap, so early on in the dime's production, she was confused with Mercury, and everyone just kind of rolled with that. Mercury dimes are readily available at coin shops and online, but if you can't get one, I promise a regular dime will work just fine.)
+ A small green bag
+ A money-drawing herb (allspice, cinnamon, or thyme)
+ Gold-colored thread
+ One other item that we'll get to in just a second

Get comfortable in front of your altar, or in your ritual space. Take up the green bag and place the dime at the bottom, then add three healthy pinches of your herb of choice.

The last item you're going to add to the bag is something uniquely representative of you.

A baby tooth would work well. You could also write out your full legal and/or magical name on a slip of paper, or draw a personal sigil, or mark a scrap of paper with a drop of your own blood. Whatever it is, it's going to adhere the spell to you, and to you alone—you are *not* to make the bag and then go, "Okay, but I have that one friend who needs this a lot more than I do…" No. *Bad Virgo*. This spell is for *you*. Don't make me get the squirt bottle.

Slide the final item down the inside of the bag, pushing it past the herbage and getting it as close to the dime as you can. Once it's settled in a way that makes sense to you, tie off the bag with the gold thread, then sprinkle it three times with salt water and run it three times through some incense smoke. To seal the spell, dip your thumb in Ivo's Virgo Anointing Oil (or, if you haven't had a chance to make it yet, *but it's definitely on your to-do list*, you can also use all-purpose olive oil) and press it into the fabric of the bag. The work is done.

Keep the bag in your pocket or purse, as close to your wallet as possible, and do your best to put it out of your mind—just let it do its job without any additional futzing on your part. But do enjoy a secret thrill whenever you come across a twenty-dollar bill on the street, or win ten bucks with a scratch-off, or find a handful of bills in the pocket of your winter coat. Because it's those little surprise payments that are ultimately going to convince you that it's just as rewarding to do magic for yourself as it is for anyone else.

The challenge here is actually casting the spell. Because when it comes to our own well-being, Virgos will plan and organize and strategize and make a list and think about how great things will be after the work is complete, to the point that we never get around to doing the work.

And this is where we can revisit the myth of Astraea, who proactively did what she needed to do to take care of herself. She shines down upon us as our Sun sign, so we can take and use that energy and emulate her by taking care of ourselves as well.

And we can also take cues from another goddess associated with Virgo: Persephone. Classical myths tell us that she was abducted by Hades, whereas modern social media versions of her legend focus on Persephone and Hades having a loving, healthy relationship. But one of the earliest-known legends of Persephone, as reconstructed by Charlene Spretnak in *Lost Goddesses of Early Greece: A Collection of Pre-Hellenic Myths* (Moon Books, 1978), depicts her making the conscious decision to enter the underworld because she had a job to do. To sum up, she did what was right for her, regardless of what her mother or future husband thought about it.

As Virgo witches, we have very clear understandings of what is right for us. So let's follow the examples set by our goddesses and actually *do* what's right for us.

Easier said than done, of course. Knowing what we should do is infinitely less stressful than taking action. Sometimes, that action won't happen until the pain of things remaining the same is greater than the pain of change. But I believe in us. Virgos are one of the most misunderstood and underestimated of the signs, so while people may see us as capable and dependable, they often don't realize just *how much* we're capable of.

Like I said earlier, we should always aspire to be the Virgos No One Saw Coming. But we can build off that to become the Virgos We Want to See in the World as well.

When I meditate on that concept, my mind immediately goes to the High Priestess who initiated me into the Gardnerian tradition, and whose birthday falls just a couple of days before mine. We were chatting about magic one day, and the subject of curses came up, and she said something that, to me, was the absolute epitome of the Virgo witch perspective:

"Oh, I never put curses on anyone … unless I *really* want to."

It was right up there with Astraea announcing, "Screw you guys; I'm going home," or Persephone being like, "This place is spooky; I'm not leaving," and it had a huge impact on the way I viewed myself as a Virgo, a witch, and a Virgo witch.

Although she prefers runes to tarot, my High Priestess keeps the Strength card from the Rider-Waite-Smith deck displayed on a bookshelf in her living room. The card has always been important to her, and while I maintain my own handicaps when it comes to tarot, the card has become important to me as well. It depicts a young woman embracing a lion, and there's a theory that the two figures represent the cusp of Leo and Virgo. What this means to me is that as a Virgo, I have access to a lot more inner strength than I am wont to give myself credit for.

As a Virgo witch, you have that inner strength to draw on as well, even when it doesn't feel like it. But it's definitely there, waiting in the wings for us to tap into it. It's there when we need to set boundaries, or when we need to rev ourselves up enough to ask for and accept help when we need it. And it's there when the last things we want to do are stop thinking and start acting.

But here's the thing: when we do finally get out of our heads and take action, especially when we're doing what's right for us, Virgo witches are damn near unstoppable. So let's put ourselves first and move forward.

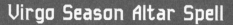

Virgo Season Altar Spell

Alexander Cabot

Born under a Virgo Sun, I always come alive during the time of what many consider the second harvest, and it's natural for me to feel at home in the September month of the Sun's annual life. I reflect on compassion and am thankful for the bounty of the year that I like to share and offer to my Goddess in her aspects as either Bride or Modron (Mabon's mother who wept for the loss of her son and looked hopefully for his return, per the Mabinogion).

Setting Up a Virgo Season Altar

Your Virgo altar is meant to honor the season in which Virgo falls, the sign's attributes, and yourself. It is a place of compassion, sharing, and thankfulness. It is where you can make offerings of the bounty of the season and give thanks for the abundance you have received throughout the year. Keep your altar small and simple; it does not have to be cumbersome and take up much space. I like to place my Virgo altar in the north due to its association with the element of earth and abundance.

+ Decorate with seasonal trimmings, such as autumnal leaves, acorns, marigold flowers, and sunflowers.

- Place basic representations of the elements: incense for air, a candle for fire, a dish of water, a dish of salt for earth. I like to use my cauldron filled with graveyard dirt, ash, and patchouli and salt.
- Set out offerings of fruits and vegetables of the season and books representing knowledge and education.
- Add items you feel represent the aspects of Virgo or those aspects you might want to focus on in the coming year.

The Spell of Virgo

You will need:
- Your altar
- Pen and paper
- Cauldron or other heat-safe dish
- Matches or lighter

With the paper and pen, write everything you have received through the year that you are thankful for. These do not have to be physical or material things to be considered abundance; sometimes the gifts we receive are much more.

Light the paper on fire and drop it into your heat-safe dish or cauldron and say,

Lady of silver, God of golden hue, bless this spell I offer you.

As the virgin Goddess in its reign has completed its solar return to attain.

I send out my petition of love, prosperity, and overall health that marks out my year

with its mercurial embrace and welcome his grace to give me the speed of light and knowledge.

Rooted in the Earth I stand with the turning of the wheel at hand.

The second harvest is upon us, with abundance in its entirety.

I call out its forces of strength and courage and

I call out the Lady who gives me input and process.

May we send out the correct energies for the good of all and harming none!

So mote it be . . .

CONCLUSION

Ivo Dominguez, Jr.

I hope you are putting what you discovered in this book to use in your witchcraft. You may have a desire to learn more about how astrology and witchcraft fit together. One of the best ways to do this is to talk about it with other practitioners. Look for online discussions, and if there is a local metaphysical shop, check to see if they have classes or discussion groups. If you don't find what you need, consider creating a study group. Learning more about your own birth chart is also an excellent next step. Some resources for study are listed in the back of this book.

At some point, you may wish to call upon the services of an astrologer to give you a reading that is fine-tuned to your chart. There are services that provide not just charts but full chart readings that are generated by software. These are a decent tool and more economical than a professional astrologer, but they lack the finesse and intuition that only a person can offer. Nonetheless, they can be a good starting point. If you do decide to hire an astrologer to do your chart, shop around to find someone attuned to your spiritual needs. You may decide to learn enough astrology to read your own chart, and that will serve you for many reasons. However, for the same reasons that tarot readers will go to someone else for a reading, the same is true with astrological readers. It is hard to see some things when you are too attached to the outcomes.

If you find your interest in astrology and its effect on a person's relationship to witchcraft has been stimulated by this book, you may wish to read the other books in this series. Additionally, if you have other witches you work with, you'll find that knowing more about how they approach their craft will make your collective efforts more productive. Understanding them better will also help reduce conflicts or misunderstandings. The ending of this book is really the beginning of the adventure.

APPENDIX
VIRGO CORRESPONDENCES

August 22/23–September 22

Symbol: ♍

Solar System: Earth, Mercury

Season: Summer

Day: Wednesday

Time of Day: Midnight

Runes: Beore, Ken

Element: Earth

Colors: Black, Blue (Navy), Brown (Dark), Gold, Gray (Dark), Green, Pink, Purple, Violet, White, Yellow

Energy: Yin

Chakras: Sacral, Solar Plexus, Throat

Number: 6, 9

Tarot: Hermit, Magician

Trees: Beech, Chestnut, Cypress, Hazel, Horse Chestnut, Maple, Mimosa, Oak, Walnut

Herb and Garden: Aster, Bergamot, Dill, Fennel, Honeysuckle, Hyacinth, Lavender, Lily, Lily of the Valley, Marjoram, Peppermint, Rosemary, Valerian, Violet

Miscellaneous Plants: Eyebright, Horehound, Patchouli, Sandalwood, Skullcap

Gemstones and Minerals: Agate, Amazonite, Amethyst, Andalusite, Apatite, Aquamarine, Aventurine, Carnelian, Chrysocolla, Diamond, Emerald, Garnet, Jade, Jasper (Pink), Lapis Lazuli, Lodestone, Moss Agate, Opal, Peridot, Sapphire, Sardonyx, Sugilite, Tourmaline (Watermelon), Tsavorite, Turquoise, Zircon (Red)

Metals: Mercury

Goddesses: Anat, Artemis, Demeter, Diana, Hestia, Inanna, Iris, Ishtar, Isis, Kore, Nanna, Persephone, Vesta

Gods: Odin

Animals: Bear (Brown), Cat, Pig (Sow), Squirrel

Birds: Sparrow

Issues, Intentions, and Powers: Abundance, Beginnings, Consciousness, Cycles, Destiny, Emotions, Endings, Grounding, Independence, Intuition, Love, the Mind (Analytical), Nurture, Order/Organize, Purification, Sexuality, Shyness, Success (Business), Well-Being

Excerpted with permission from *Llewellyn's Complete Book of Correspondences: A Comprehensive & Cross-Referenced Resource for Pagans & Wiccans* © 2013 by Sandra Kynes.

RESOURCES

Online

Astrodienst: Free birth charts and many resources.

+ https://www.astro.com/horoscope

Astrolabe: Free birth chart and software resources.

+ https://alabe.com

The Astrology Podcast: A weekly podcast hosted by professional astrologer Chris Brennan.

+ https://theastrologypodcast.com

Magazine

The Mountain Astrologer: The world's most recognized astrology magazine. Available in print and digital formats.

+ https://mountainastrologer.com

Books

+ *Practical Astrology for Witches and Pagans* by Ivo Dominguez, Jr.
+ *Parkers' Astrology: The Definitive Guide to Using Astrology in Every Aspect of Your Life* by Julia and Derek Parker

- *The Inner Sky: How to Make Wiser Choices for a More Fulfilling Life* by Steven Forrest
- *Predictive Astrology: Tools to Forecast Your Life and Create Your Brightest Future* by Bernadette Brady
- *Chart Interpretation Handbook: Guidelines for Understanding the Essentials of the Birth Chart* by Stephen Arroyo
- *Cunningham's Encyclopedia of Magical Herbs* by Scott Cunningham
- *The Treadwell's Book of Plant Magic* by Christina Oakley Harrington
- *Pagan Portals—The Art of Lithomancy: Divination with Stones, Crystals, and Charms* by Jessica Howard
- *Lithomancy: Divination and Spellcraft with Stones, Crystals, and Coins* by Rev. Dr. Jon Saint Germain
- *Lost Goddesses of Early Greece: A Collection of Pre-Hellenic Myths* by Charlene Spretnak

CONTRIBUTORS

We give thanks and appreciation to all our guest authors who contributed their own special Virgo energy to this project.

Stephanie Rose Bird

Stephanie Rose Bird has written several books, including the award-winning and bestselling *Sticks, Stones, Roots & Bones* and *365 Days of Hoodoo*. Her book *Four Seasons of Mojo* is being republished as *African American Magick* by Weiser soon. Bird is an eclectic pagan practicing shamanism, green witchcraft, and hoodoo. She, her husband, family, and animals live in Chicagoland. Visit her at http://www.stephanierosebird.com.

Alexander Cabot

Involved with several magickal traditions since childhood, and a traditionalist at heart, Rev. Alexander Cabot represents Gardnerian/New York Wica from the Kentucky Line through Lady Rhea, the Welsh from Eddie Buczynski, and the Cabot Tradition from Laurie Cabot of Salem, Massachusetts.

Ellen Dugan

Ellen Dugan is the award-winning author of forty-two books and the *Witches Tarot*. She branched out successfully into paranormal fiction in 2015. Her portfolio of work also includes fifteen nonfiction magickal books and twenty-five novels. Ellen is a psychic-clairvoyant and has been a practicing Witch for over thirty-five years.

Dawn Aurora Hunt

Dawn Aurora Hunt, owner of Cucina Aurora Kitchen Witchery, is the author of *A Kitchen Witch's Guide to Love & Romance* and *Kitchen Witchcraft for Beginners*. Though not born under the sign of Virgo, she combines knowledge of spiritual goals and magickal ingredients to create recipes for all Sun signs in this series. She is a Scorpio. Find her at www .CucinaAurora.com.

Sandra Kynes

Sandra Kynes (Midcoast Maine) is the author of nineteen books, including *Mixing Essential Oils for Magic*, *Magical Symbols and Alphabets*, *Crystal Magic*, *Plant Magic*, and *Sea Magic*. Excerpted content from her book, *Llewellyn's Complete Book of Correspondences*, has been used throughout this series. She is a Scorpio. Find her at http://www.kynes.net.

Gina Martini

Gina has been a working pagan since 1986; she has expanded her studies to many forms of witchcraft, ritual magic shamanism and wisewoman work, trance movement, Norse, Buddhism, and nature reverence. Since then, she has developed her own form of paganism, Walking in Magic. She still confesses to know no thing…

Mercedes NineMoons

Mercedes NineMoons comes from an unbroken matriarchal line of creole Orisa/Ifa rootworkers.

She is a creatrix, artist, 2nd Degree Cabot Priestess, Curandera, and a Master Alchemical Herbalist. She is the driving force behind Bruja Coffee + Apothecary Co., a Latina- and Woman-owned company. Visit her at https://bruja-coffee-co.myshopify.com.

Katrina Rasbold

Katrina Rasbold is the author of more than thirty-five books, including *Uncrossing* (Llewellyn, 2021) and a fictional series called *The Sisters of Avalon*. She and her husband own Crossroads Occult (www.crossroadsoccult.com), offering magical services and handmade products. She has studied the magical arts in England, Mexico, and throughout the United States.

Notes

Notes

Notes

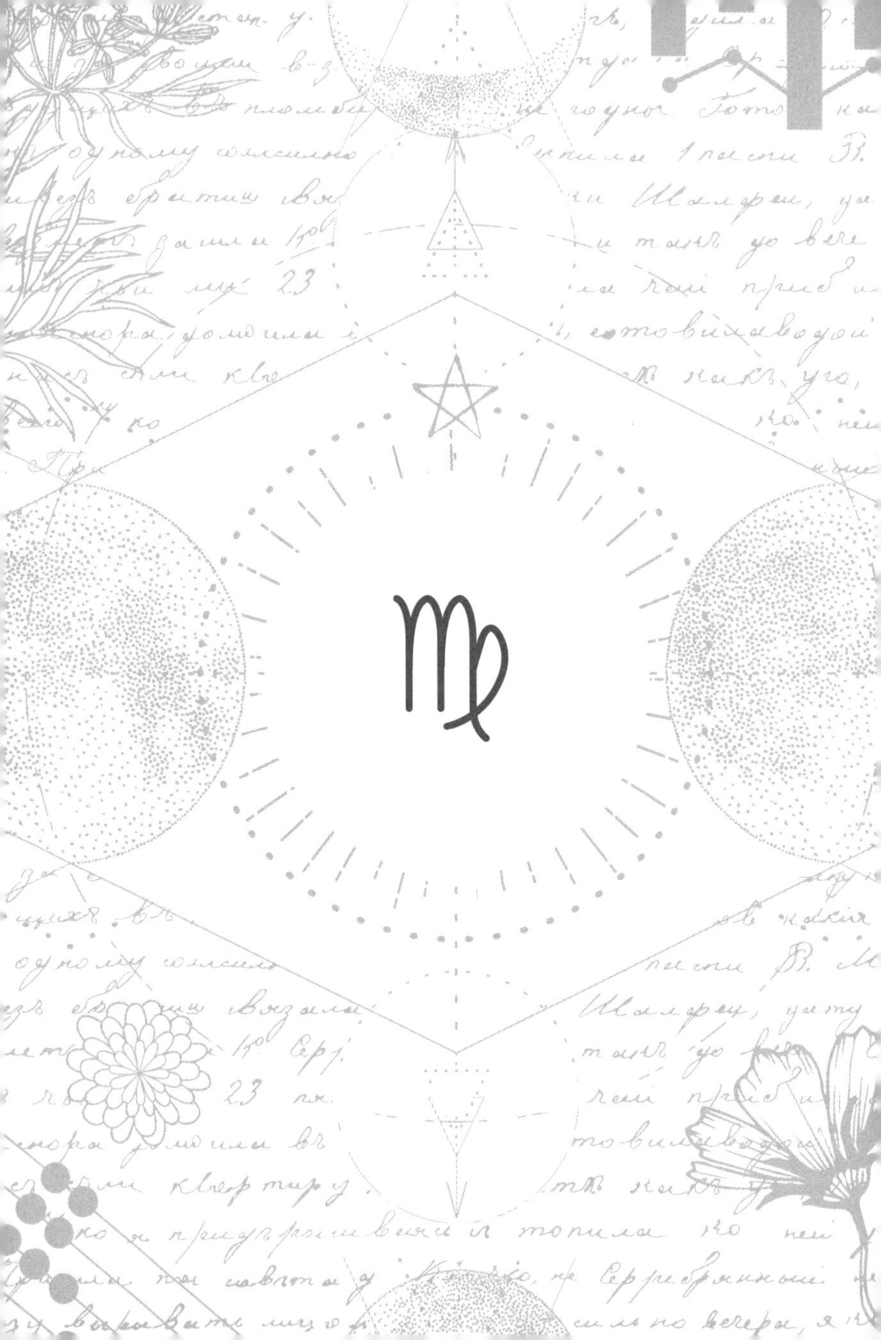

To Write to the Author

If you wish to contact the author or would like more information about this book, please write to the author in care of Llewellyn Worldwide Ltd. and we will forward your request. Both the author and the publisher appreciate hearing from you and learning of your enjoyment of this book and how it has helped you. Llewellyn Worldwide Ltd. cannot guarantee that every letter written to the author can be answered, but all will be forwarded. Please write to:

Ivo Dominguez, Jr.
Thumper Forge
℅ Llewellyn Worldwide
2143 Wooddale Drive
Woodbury, MN 55125-2989

Please enclose a self-addressed stamped envelope for reply, or $1.00 to cover costs. If outside the U.S.A., enclose an international postal reply coupon.

Many of Llewellyn's authors have websites with additional information and resources. For more information, please visit our website at:

www.llewellyn.com